THE PORTRAIT

THE PORTRAIT

SECRETS, LIES, AND REVELATIONS

*UNDER THE AUSPICIOUS NAME OF
CARTER ZEGERS GALLAGHER*

*AN INTIMATE LOOK INTO THE
THOUGHTS AND DESIRES OF AN ARTIST*

WORDS BY:
Melvin Montemayor Martinez

iUniverse, Inc.
New York Lincoln Shanghai

THE PORTRAIT
SECRETS, LIES, AND REVELATIONS

iUniverse, Inc.

For information address:
iUniverse, Inc.
2021 Pine Lake Road, Suite 100
Lincoln, NE 68512
www.iuniverse.com

ISBN: 0-595-27430-7 (pbk)
ISBN: 0-595-74663-2 (cloth)

Printed in the United States of America

WITH LOVE

RUBEN AND BELEN MARTINEZ

ALSO

MY BROTHERS AND SISTER

FOR

CONRAD VILLAREAL,

**WHO FIRST SHOWED ME HOW TO EXPRESS MYSELF
THROUGH THE POWER OF WORDS**

LASTLY

GOD ALMIGHTY

FOR GIVING ME THE GIFT OF WRITING

THERE IS NO SUCH THING AS A PROBLEM

WITHOUT A GIFT FOR YOU IN ITS HANDS,

YOU ARE NEVER GIVEN A WISH

WITHOUT ALSO BEING GIVEN THE POWER TO MAKE IT

COME TRUE.

—CONRAD VILLAREAL

MAY THE ROAD RISE TO MEET YOU,

MAY THE WIND BE ALWAYS AT YOUR BACK,

THE SUN SHINE WARM UPON YOUR FACE,

THE RAIN FALL SOFT UPON YOUR FIELDS,

AND UNTIL WE MEET AGAIN...

MAY GOD HOLD YOU IN THE HOLLOW OF HIS HANDS.

—MARCELO SION

YOU MAY SEARCH HIGH AND LOW

FOR THE THINGS THAT YOU SEEK AND CRAVE.

BUT IT PALES IN COMPARISON TO THE ONE

THAT HE WILL OFFER YOU.

HIS LOVE.

UNDYING AND UNLIMITED

—MELVIN MARTINEZ

I LOVE YOU SO MUCH!!!

—MOM

Contents

A JOURNEY...

The moment is at hand, for me to realize that my destiny awaits. To live the life that has been given to me by the power that is above all. Though mine is just starting to unfold, revealing some signs that will enable me to pursue the events that will lead to my own salvation. Knowing that I will eventually lead a life of satisfaction, without fear and hesitation, or would it only cause more damage from the sheer weight of responsibility that I had to carry knowing that what lies ahead is something that would eventually lead to my own destruction. To realize that the future is nowhere near the one that I intend to partake, rather an unseen force is at hand, manipulating the events and shaping them into their own twisted desire. With no clear notion, whether the decisions I make and the paths I take are really mine to begin with. On the other hand, is it just another plot in the unending series of fate that has been bestowed upon me? It's all up to me now, to view how things in my life would come into fruition. To trust myself enough that everything will fall into place and in the end comes knowledge and wisdom that I alone have attained through experience and learning.

I have reached an epiphany where I am but a mere foot soldier to the vastness of unending struggle to be somebody. To belong and to have someone share that special something you keep on holding onto so dearly. To love and loved in return. Through the difficulties and struggles that I've encountered, the endless sacrifices and oppressions that seems so boundless, and through the joyful times and proud moments I've experienced, all these and more I give you the pleasure of knowing what I went through and how someone like me can become somebody that shows real emotions where anyone can relate to. To experience the life I had. Moreover, maybe learn from it. I am happy with what became of my life. The experiences that I alone encountered are in itself treasures that will stay on with me forever.

Like pictures that holds the moment of one's life, forever sealing them in a piece of treasure that will eventually be a part of their past. My life, also, represents portraits of events that captured every struggle, every triumph, and every emotion I have gone through. Moments in time, that has become an integral part of my being, that without a piece of it, I can never be complete. Each portrait tells a story on how I came to be, on how I use the life that has been handed down to me, and of how I will forever be grateful for everything that has happened to me.

This is my story. Come and take a peak into my own **Portraits...**

1

A PEN IS MIGHTIER THAN A SWORD

Something tells me that this is going to be one hell of explaining to do. I am not so sure where to start, or how to even start it. The way I see it, every time I begin to write something out of context, somewhere beneath the surface of an unbreakable exterior, where simple meaning might mean a thousand words, I could never attain such magnitude of intensity unless such heart wrenching feelings of sadness envelops me. It is by far the one thing that has made me do what I do best, writing. Although, I feel validated about writing in such a foul disposition, considering the fact that through this form of medium, I can truly voice out my opinions towards someone and something no matter what the outcome. To let everything out in you escape neither by shouting nor by screaming from the top of your voice, but rather in a gentler, subtler way of doing it. Writing is definitely a passion of mine. It has been for as long as I can remember, even before I discovered that I also have the gift of creating empty canvases into eye-catching landscapes and astonishing picturesque views. In addition, even though I am constantly reminding myself that I can never be a Danielle Steele or a Stephen King, who are both bestsellers when it comes to writing romantic novels and science fictions, respectively. Nor will I ever be a Conrad V. or a Marcelo S., who both can write words so intricate and meaningful, one needs to be a walking thesaurus in order for them to understand the true purpose of what they are implying. Simple and yet complicated. That's what they are, it's a shame I can never be like them. I am and will always be a simple writer creating stories and putting simple words to convey meaningful expressions.

I guess I have a special way of knowing what and how people think and feel about one another in a way that I don't have to look at them in order to find out whether there is a sense of hatred or joy in their eyes. Then putting those emotions into words where everyone can relate to. For others, they may find it rather boring and inconsequential to sit down in a corner and do nothing except letting their fingers do the work. While to some, they enjoy a moment's peace and tranquility where minds benefit and new experiences are discovered. It is usually at this moment that they realize that what they have started may end up something more than what they have expected. A novel, a short story, an essay, or even a poem, whatever they might call it. To me, I call it a **masterpiece.** It's something to feel good about, to look back at the time when something like that was created and to remember how it feels like knowing that you have created a masterpiece through a simple form called writing.

Yes, writing is indeed, to me, a therapy. For it not only let me express my own emotions about how and what I feel towards others and how and what they feel towards me, but also, in many occasions, has somehow soothe my soul with utmost clarity. It made me re-think and re-assess about everything that surrounds me, to learn and relearn from my mistakes, and to make sure to jot down everything I feel and see. However, don't get me wrong, it's pretty hard to put words into writing much more knowing exactly what you feel while coming up with a word that matches with what you are experiencing. But I wonder if the marks that I've left behind, like the footprints in the sand, or the stains on the shirt, even still the words and emotions I've expressed would leave a mark of inspiration for others or just create a devastating scar to the persons that have been part of my life. If so, I only wish that I could take back the words that I've said, the feelings I've expressed and the scars I've created. For I know that no one has to suffer from someone else's mistakes and only to be repaid by creating another one.

I know this for I have live it.

2

HIDDEN TREASURE

There are rare moments that my attention deviates from the current problems clouding my mind. Moments when alone in a place far away from all the source of my problems that seems so impossible to solve, where only you and the surroundings that nature can offer dwells. Where you are nowhere near the aches and pains that seems to find its way and crawl relentlessly towards the unsuspecting you. To get away from it all, it does sounds good to have something like that. Yet it can happen, it can bring out the one thing from within you that has been kept dormant for a long time, wanting to be let out of its cage and reach you from the depths of its core. Finally, you let everything out. The sadness, the anger, the frustrations, everything that has left you crippled and maimed. All that is left is happiness. Happy that you finally let yourself feel differently other than the ones you keep on holding onto. Glad that you have something more within you than what has been constantly dominating your life. You see, once in a complete of state of grace, nobody's there but you, nobody's there to tell you what to do and where to go, and nobody's there to interrupt you on moments when you reminisce all the fond memories you shared with your loved ones, your friends. A sense of wanting to bring everything back the way they use to, the way they were. Somehow, you want them to see, to hear, to feel and even smell the things you're experiencing right now, right at this very moment. Maybe, even have some laughs and silly discussions among the people your comfortable being with. Yet you know that you can never have everything back the way you want it, so instead you opt for something second best and that is finding a place where you can be alone and be yourself. A place you can call yours. You need not go to a place as grand as the Taj Mahal or as magnificent as the pyramids just to find a place that you can relate. A place as simple as a park is perfectly suited for anyone and everyone who seeks refuge from the burden that life brings. It's a place booming with people from all walks of life, that in the morning through late afternoon, it's a place of loud noises, crowding with kids playing, parents watch-

3

ing and siblings teasing and horsing around with each other. Yet at night at around six and eight pm, when the moon is just starting to show its awe-inspiring luminescence, surrounding every corner with its mixtures of red and yellow hues, with a touch of orange and purple rays. And from a far, crickets singing their tunes of mating, and those wonderful creatures that light up the skies, blinking every time a potential mate passes by, hoping that somehow in the midst of darkness, they could still find their way to each of them. Looking at this scenery is like watching an orchestra perform their favorite symphony. The place itself instantaneously transforms into this marvelous scenery of peace, hope and most of all, happiness. This is my place, a place I can call my own, so to speak.

Anyway, once in this place and in the complete state of calmness and peace, you will then find something else inside of you that has been there all along but unaware of its existence because it has been locked away deep within your psyche. Now it wants to be felt, to be let out of its darkened cell. Where all your dreams, hopes, aspirations live. Your future reaches out to your very soul wanting to be needed, to be recognized. Then you realize that these are the things to come, things that you've always dreamed of. Moreover, the only person who can make it happen is you. That you alone can fulfill your dreams and desires in this life and nobody else could take that away from you not even if they take it by force or by manipulation. It is as they say, "You are given a free will, and with it comes responsibilities." It is how you deal with such responsibility that makes you who you are. You can't let anyone strap you down, or tell you what to do while holding you at the end of some short leash. Your dream of becoming somebody, your hopes of having something and sharing it with your special someone. These are a part of you, of what you really are. Deep inside of you its there waiting to be needed and wanted, but sometimes it gets buried when complications arises and your attention deviates from reaching your goals.

Nevertheless, whenever you feel as though everything seems to fall apart, simple things becoming increasingly out of hand, indecisive and simply confused. Remember that there will always be a place that you could go and let everything fall into place, arranging them into whatever style you want them to be.

Such moments maybe a rarity, lasting only in minutes, but the experience will last forever. This I can guarantee.

3

RUDE AWAKENING

Life maybe compared to a spider's web, full of intricacies and complex machinations, that we sometimes forget that we are the ones who weave our life, our web life. Is it not true that like a spider's web with its perfectly woven parts, and not so perfectly woven parts intertwined with one another like minute representations of the life we now lead? One webbing overlapping another indicating that in one significant moment of our life we decided not to do anything except stand still, hoping that that particular event would fade away and never to come back. Frozen in time, unaware that we still need to do something or anything to keep ourselves going…

Ha! It's intriguing how people will resort to hide behind their intellect, in order to ignore what is pretty obvious from the very beginning, emotions.

I made it all up, the web of life, the intertwining parts and decision crap! No, I didn't read it at some fancy literary book or even see it on television, but rather it's a product of my higher reasoning to ignore what I am truly feeling inside. To let my emotions ran rampant outside the normal perception of others. Believe me I'm neither the first one who's been in this situation before nor will I ever be the last one. Many people are in the same situation as I am, about being somewhat antsy when it comes to their emotions, especially revealing it to others. I just hope that nobody reads this crap and go on telling others what has happened to me and the emotions I've expressed. Nobody wants to hear that, not even me.

However, what and how do I really feel? Have I been stalling by writing senseless explanations just to avoid this subject? Try reading the part where I'm describing life as a spider's web, go on…read it.

What did I tell you? Truth is, I know what and how I am feeling and somehow I still have the inclination not to put it in writing. It's hard to put feelings into words, much more if you hear those words spoken to you and you don't like what is being said about you, especially when those words are coming from your father. Complaining, nagging, and hurting your feelings. I don't know him that well since he left to the States to find a better way of living for his family when I was just ten years old. He left to make sure that our life wouldn't be the same as his was when he was growing up, where food, money, and opportunity are very scarce. One thing I do know while spending time with him during my first formative years of my life was he instilled in our hearts the word FEAR. To him, everything that you do has to be perfectly done, arranged, and executed, otherwise, if it doesn't conform to his standards, you will hear the most annoying and hurtful sound the world has ever produced. The sound that would also leave a scar so deep it pierces your very soul-the sound of hatred. I find myself wondering who the person that stares back at me. Has he changed that much since he left? Have I repressed so much memories of him that I have forgotten all along what he was like? On the other hand, is this a manifestation of what he has become and I never really realized it up until now.

I am living with him in a place not foreign to me. Expecting to have a warm and loving home waiting for us at the end of long trip that ended with us leaving our past behind to start a new life, and after ten years of establishing himself, thinking that we can all now be together and remembering all the fond days we shared back then. There was none. Except a house with people I don't know. People that only now have I been informed about their relationship with my father. A new place in a new house, living with a new family not my own. It's an experience that overwhelmed me.

One must realize that this is very unusual for someone like me, especially after being educated and experienced about the close-knit relationship that has been part of our lives for as long as I've been living. I know that the world is changing and the people living in that world will eventually change or adapt with their environment as well, for better or worse, I have no idea. However, what I do know is, after ten long years of being separated from each other, missing our birthdays and graduations', knowing that he is by himself with no one to comfort and care for him and always thinking about us. That when we finally are reunited, it's all going to be just us, nobody else. A family reunited together, if not completely. I can only say that now I am beginning to realize that coming here and staying with him and his new family may not be a good idea to begin with. I have nothing here, no one to talk to, no one to ask for help and nobody to give me guidance and respect. The minute he sees a mistake, a flaw in our performance, he'll jump at you, your ears will be ringing for days, and the worst part is that these words are coming from none other than your father. A father who should be loving you instead of saying horrible things, supporting you instead of degrading and ruining your life. Such a shame that the only time I am happy in this house I live in are at times when he is away at work. Most days I don't even want to go down from my room upstairs and dine with them at dinner. I just let them know that dinner is ready after I prepare and set everything for them. Sometimes he'll ask why I'm not dining with them, and I'll say that I am not hungry and to go ahead and not worry about me. Which is of course is not true. I am hungry. They don't know this but it's true.

There are days that I cannot even count on my fingers how many times I go hungry, starving for that matter. Afraid to go down and join them whenever their out there, so I jut let myself wait 'til they decided to go somewhere else besides their room. If they do decided to go out, it usually tells me that it's safe to go down and have something to eat, or to quench my thirst. I am a prisoner in my own room, so to speak. I've never liked doing this, taking my food up to my room or in any part of the house for that matter, except the dining room of course, simply because I've been taught about the right manners of properly knowing where to dine with your food. Nevertheless, I am forced to do it largely because of the fact that dining with them would mean that I have to pretend to be okay which I'm not. I chose not to dine with them also for the reason of not being criticized by them through words and through their constant staring, as though you are no better than anyone of them. I could not take such a punch like that, not from him or anybody else.

I never knew he was like this, but if I did, somehow I would never have come here in the first place. He hasn't change, I still remember him back then of what he was like and I guess until now he still bear the same mark of the father who likes to nag and complain about a lot of things and about everybody. Paranoia of some sort magnified to the nth degree the moment we set foot on this house, and the moment he found out how different we are from what he perceived us to be. He thought that we were these perfectly trained, educated kids that can never mess up in everything we do. He got disappointed, I guess. Then he starts blaming the one person responsible for taking care of us, my mom. On how she raised us, how irresponsible, narrow-minded woman she is. That's all I hear from him. To me, my mom did her best in raising five kids, who are all boys, budgeting the money my father sends us after, I think, splitting it between his two families. She also helped us with our home works and countless school projects, and most of all, keeping us from troubles. I never see him do that with his newfound family, he lets me teach my half-sister of the things to do at home and at school. I really don't mind doing this; of course, I love her very much. I hope she knows that. This way I could also teach her what my mom taught me on how to look at the world with confidence. However, the minute he finds a flaw in my sister's work, that she has not been living up to his standards. Whom do you think is blamed for that? Me! Just like when he blames my mom for every little flaw that we make. All the hate, all the finger pointing at us, at my mom, blaming us for everything.

It's sad. It breaks my heart to know that such foul words and hatred comes from the person that we respected the most, the one I love the most, my father.

4

SINS OF THE FATHER

It never ends! Why is it that whenever I feel good about myself and all the things around me, there's this eerie feeling inside me that warns me that something is brewing within these walls I call home? That after all the things I do around here and the work I meticulously labored for them to be happy, it is never enough. My day always ends with a lot of complaints and dissatisfaction from the people I'm living with. What have I done to deserve this? Are these the punishments and sufferings I'm destined to have for all the sins I've done. That knowingly doing the things I did in the past, the things I've committed and the words I've uttered and the thoughts I've had are all a part of what was supposed to be this moment. I defied the very nature that what defines me as a person of morals and dignity; instead, I gave in to temptation and turned away from my faith, my religion and most of all, my entire God.

Conscience, guilt and religion are very strong combinations to overpower against such a diminutive person like me. May be I still have a chance to redeem myself from all this. A priest once told me that no matter how difficult things may be, no matter what the consequences and trials you may face, that not once in your heart believe that God is vengeful, for He is not. Moreover, I believe that truthfully. I pray every night for Him to forgive me for all the sins I've committed and for the things I have no courage to stay away from, hoping that He can hear my plight and save me from despair. I never really offered myself to Him, knowing that it's okay for me not to be perfect, that I'm only human capable of making mistakes. However, like any other person in my situation, I crumble. I'm not strong enough to resist and be true to myself. I am weak, and getting weaker every day as I face the difficulties and problems that seems be a form of a test on my part whether I am strong enough to handle such difficulty. To find out if my faith is as strong as He believes it should be. I hope I am not losing this battle since I may not last any longer. Everyday that I face the people I am living with is a struggle that makes me less of a person and a son to a father I hold dearly. To hear from him that the things we do around here is not enough, that we are not earning our keep, and we can never be responsible enough to handle a simple situation.

Now this, complaints from his so-called wife that I'm hearing, although she's not saying it directly to our faces, we could still see it by the way she moves around the house and her attitude towards us. She'd rather tell my father the things were doing wrong than admit that all we are doing was for their satisfaction. So much anger and hurt I'm feeling right now that I am not sure if I can keep it all bottled up for as long as I can, or if I can keep myself from going insane. Don't they understand that this is neither our place nor our home? I can't do anything around here that would satisfy them. I don't know why, I just can't. Maybe I'm so afraid to mess up and let her see me touching their belongings, or maybe I'm afraid to let her find out that all I did was stay up in my room, waiting for them to leave so I could then do the chores. I can't explain exactly why I'm feeling this way nevertheless, this is how I feel. Every moment since I've been here all I do is stay in my room, out of everybody's sight. To let them know that they can do anything they want and all they have to do is leave me alone!

Each passing day, whenever one of them comes home after a long days work, I always ask myself the same question every single time that has become part of my routine the moment they step into their house; is the house clean enough for them? Is everything set to their standards? I always have that gut feeling inside me of being afraid whenever one of them is at home. Afraid that I'll hear them talking about me, or just thinking that their talking about me. I'm too paranoid to think of anything else but this, afraid that I might lose my sanity over this. Please let it end now, I need to get out of this place and have my own. I need to have my own things and be my own my person. But nobody's out there to give me a helping hand. I have nothing…except a prayer and a little hope that despite all this, everything will be all right. I pray…

"Oh God, with your merciful hand and loving heart, please give me your guidance and support that I may know what to do in times of hardship and despair. Help me overcome temptation and know what is right and what is wrong when it's time for me to decide what path to take and what decision to make, and I hope that You'll find it in Your heart to forgive me for the horrible things that I have done. I also pray that You'll forever stay with me for the rest of my life, and protect me from danger, keep me safe and from harm. Lastly, remember me in Your heart, mind and in Your soul always. Amen."

5

SUNSHINE AFTER THE STORM

Do you hear that? Silence, calmness, for once it is here. Everything's back to the way it should be, for now. I have no idea how long this is going to last, a day or two maybe, I don't know, if I'm lucky it'll probably stay like this for a week, but whatever it takes I will enjoy every single moment of it.

I'm most afraid of this part. I'm not sure what it is, but I know that something is happening, waiting to be unleashed upon me. I can only expect that it won't be a pleasant one since nothing ever ends up the way I want it. If I ever have a day where everything seems to fall into place, where everybody is in perfect harmony, and a moment where every single fiber of my being is in constant sync with the elements, I probably would be in heaven, enjoying what perfection can offer. But alas, I am not there, the feeling is short-lived, for the good things are predictably followed by bad ones. I really do try my best to be happy, even for just a moment. But every time I think of what they might be saying behind my back, whether I'm having the time of my life, enjoying every little bit of what life gives me, and on the other hand, they don't. That they are the ones doing all the work without any help from me. Throwing a 'dagger' look that would certainly crush someone like me. It seems like no matter what I do, no matter how much I care or not, no matter what the outcome the day brings, the result is always the same. In the end, I'm always alone, and most importantly, sad. Sad that I can't do anything in this place. Thinking that I should also suffer, not being able to enjoy and have fun within these walls I call home, and as well as out there where an abundance of opportunity awaits, I stay behind. Not because I want to, but rather because of the situation and the circumstances that has befallen my unfortunate life. I unintentionally do this in order for them to know that I, too, am suffering as they are. I have somewhat created a façade of deception wherein I am trying to fit into their personas. Hence, when they're happy, I am happy, when their suffering from whatever reason, I, too am suffering.

Yet the truth behind such deception is the reality that I am in need of help. A helping hand to lift up my spirit and bring salvation to my suffering, for I suffer dearly, not from lack of food or resources that are surely plentiful, but from the life I am leading. A life that I am not in control of. Were it not for the love and respect that I have for my father, I would have taken the life that they meticulously manipulated and taken advantage of with severe vengeance. Not that I was going to kill myself, if that was some people's interpretation, but to take away their control over me, hurtful words and physical violence may have erupted if I were to go through with it. To take back what is rightfully mine, yet logic and fear of being alone prevented me from doing anything. Therefore, I stay and serve.

This is what has become of me. What I do is not to my own accord. A prisoner and an occupant in a place full of discoveries and experiences, yet I have no idea what's out there. To find out what lies ahead, I need to sever the ties that bind me into this place. Until I have the courage to undo what has been done to me, to rightfully correct the mistakes made by others in my name, I will stay. But this time, it will be different, this I promise.

There's always a calm before the storm. The storm is coming. I am the storm. Hear me roar!

6

A SKELETON IN THE CLOSET

Being and coming here may not be the best thing that ever happened to me. Opportunities may be boundless, new ideas can be worth a fortune, or let's just say that reuniting with the family you've 'lost' for almost twelve years, that it might soften the heart of a hard man, maybe even dropping to his knees weeping, not for sadness nor despair, but for joyful reconciliation with his love ones. Such event can surely make anyone shed a teardrop, only to wipe it away, so as not to let anyone see him cry. Unfortunately, it never happened. As it turned out, coming to this place has only brought me more harm than good. I thought coming here, living with the father, who as far as I could recall has been a constant inspiration to me, and the one I longed to be with since the day he left home to pursue a life for his children that will eventually lead to our reconciliation and togetherness. Hoping that the moment we arrived would mark a beginning of a new relationship between father and son, a reunification of some sort. Between him, his family and us, but as always, I was wrong. Then again, it doesn't surprise me though; it was something I would have expected, even predicted. You see, from the time when we were kids, all I could remember was this big strapping man that always had a reputation of getting moody whatever and whenever there is something wrong, may it be from the way the house looks like or the way his children behave. Even the slightest flaw, a mistake, or a dot on a perfectly clean white piece of paper, he would start flaring up. Not just for a moment but for as long as he can remember. And that is what makes him very dangerous, for he will let you know what you've done, when you've done it, and he will make you feel very small for doing it. To the point that guilt overcomes your other emotions. Moreover, there's nothing else you can do, but feel sorry for yourself, funny thing is, it's not from what you've done, rather its how he made you feel about yourself.

Fear is another thing he's good at. Never have I remembered that a day goes by that we weren't fearful of him. You can never make a mistake when you're around him, otherwise, I'm not saying that he physically abuses us, or me, that's nothing compared to where it really hurts-inside. His words are like sharp knives that pierce deep within your soul, he aims directly through my heart. I never have the courage to talk back, to let him know that what's his doing is hurting me. I just can't. I have nothing here to back me up, compared to when I was back home, even if I talk back at my mom, voicing out my opinions, even to the point of disobeying her and making her really mad at me, I know for a fact that she still loves me despite my shortcomings. She'll always be there no matter what and she'll support you all the way. But when it comes to my father, I'm afraid that I'll end up in the streets, with no one and nowhere to go but down in the gutters. I did it once, you know, talk back and it made him more angry and disappointed and hurtful towards me, which me made realize that he didn't love me at all.

I've never been happy since I set foot on this place, a place I'd like to call my home. One might suggest, why not just go back home? Why not leave? Pack up my bags and return to the place I'm most happy, hoping never to look back, leaving behind the sufferings and despair.

I can't. As hard as it may sound, I just can't. I don't know why, maybe, I don't want to start all over again. Maybe this is where I'm supposed to be. All I know is ever since I was young, I've always dreamed of being here, that somehow I belong here. That this is where I am destined to live my life, where I could also give my love ones back home the life we never had. Not that the one I had back home wasn't satisfying; it was in actuality an experience I would never part with. We had days that most families had, living in a tight budget, and plenty of kids around that sometimes food were not adequate enough to feed everybody, struggling to make ends meet. There were days that I wished that I was born with a different family and not have the one I have. However, that feeling quickly subsides once I know that we'll be okay as long as we have each other and that were happy with what we have. That's the same feeling I want here, where I know I am safe in the loving arms of my father and the new family he has. That is what I longed for. Is that too much to ask? To simply know that his there whenever I need him. Happiness doesn't happen often around this house, maybe that's why their like that or maybe I just focus too much on the negative things. Maybe if I were in their shoes, I would feel the same way, and would probably act the same way towards a bunch of people whom they see as someone as irresponsible as we do. They might feel that I take everything for granted and not think of the outcome before I do the things I do. This may be true; it's possible. However, it's difficult to pinpoint the exact reason why they do what they do to me, when one dominates the other, all the rest are left behind and you have no idea what will happen next. It is as if the only solution for me is to shut down everything out from the inside and let myself feel nothing, nothing at all. Even at times when everybody's seems to get along so well, I just close my eyes and tell myself that it's not happening, that it's not real. On the other hand, what if it is? I know that this is wrong of me to do, but I do it anyway, in order to protect myself from ever getting hurt again. I pretend I put on a face. When something sounds funny, I laugh with them, and when things get serious, I act an emotion that calls for it. I'm getting good at this and if this goes on forever, I might be an expert on this pretend thing. Yet somehow I am not sure about this, I mean, come on, what if they really do care about me, what if they really are interested to know what's going on with my life? I do feel like that, that they do care about me, especially my father whenever he comes up to my room and wants to have a chat with his son. Where he ask me what's up with me lately, things that a father and a son usually do on their spare time, just to catch up on things since we hardly see each other due to work related things. We talk and yet we don't really know each other, it's like a stranger is sitting in front of me, asking all this questions that I'm not sure how to answer. I am not accustomed to this. Right now, it feels different, why; I have no idea, since we never did show how we feel for each other, especially to our father. I'm not used to this kind of situation and I don't know how I should act in front of him even though it's just the two of us, which is what I've ever wanted, and yet somewhere along the way, I realize that it was never like this even back then. I was too young to have a decent conversation with my father, I was just ten years old and to have something to talk about back then would probably involve asking for toys and superheroes, or letting me stay up a little longer to watch a show that I love, and not the ones I have in mind. Therefore, whenever he wants to talk to me, I just say the things that he wants to hear. It's not being rude or anything, it seems inappropriate to let him know everything that usually I keep to myself, things that I don't want to divulge, and things I don't want him to find out. I have secrets to keep and to talk about it would only bring more problems than solution.

Maybe, this is what he misses the most. The chance to have something important to talk about or do with his children, maybe his trying to make up for lost time, to be the kind of father he always wanted to be; loving, caring and understanding. The kind where his kids jump at the chance to spend time with their wonderful father, to see the love in their children's eyes, to give as well as receive the love he so desperately missing. Maybe, he, too, may not be the only one who's new at this. Probably, his trying to find his way back into our hearts, into our loving arms, longing for an embrace from his long 'lost' children, and to comfort each other and let everyone know that everything's going to be all right. Although, hugs and kisses were present upon our first arrival, a few words of comfort said to ease each other's longing, but other than that, there were no real emotions involved, as though strangers met for the very first time in their lives.

Is this what happens when families grow apart from each other? Unfamiliar and unable to recognize that the persons standing right in front of you, is the one that you use to know and still love, probably, somewhat reluctant or unwilling to take the first step in getting closer to that person. Somehow, he might feel that he has failed us. He wasn't there when we needed him the most, when at times we call out his name, just to open our eyes and not see him there. It was hard for all of us, missing our birthdays, graduations; the fruit of his hard work, his presence alone was surely missed. He missed a lot of it since he worked repeatedly just to make sure that we had the right education, that we won't grow illiterate and not know what the world may offer us and most importantly, grow to be the person we ought to be. Missing them surely have made him so upset and depressed. He may have provided us with the necessary financial support that we needed to get through the days, nevertheless, not being there to witness the product of all the hard work he has done, it's something he could not bear. He was sad not to see us grow up and be somebody, I can't blame him for feeling that way, for he has done nothing wrong.

My father made us what we are today. If not for him, we wouldn't be here at all; he has given us qualities that surely will be a part of us for as long we are alive. I've learned that with each day that I grow, I have responsibilities and obligations that I need to accomplish, making sure that everyone in my stead are well taken care of from the food we eat to the little things that we need. That is what he has bestowed upon me, and the knowledge that, even though he may not always be there for us, presently guiding our path to success and supporting us in our failures, he will remain present in our hearts no matter where we are and whatever we choose to have in our life. And to remember that he never gave up on us for he wanted us to have everything he never had growing up.

Lastly, to face life with courage and certainty, and to never give up when things seem so confusing. To know that there's always someone to lend you a hand when you are down and alone.

However, how can I face life with nobody to share it with?

I have been alone almost from the day I discovered that I am different...

7

CONTROL

I really tried my best, I really did. However, it seems that no matter what I do, no matter how hard I try, there seems to be a bad aura hanging over my head that repels people I like the most. There are times when I meet someone I like and got a chance to know them, to the point of really falling over them, and all of a sudden, poof, and their gone. I try calling them on the phone and talk for a few minutes, trying to convince them that I can be what they want me to be. Somebody they like, someone they can go out with, to hang out with, even becoming their best friend. Heck, I'll even let them use me so they can get their own way, even if it means totally disagreeing with whatever they're doing. I'm at a focal point in my life that having somebody to share the life you cherish through its harvest and drought is as important as breathing itself. I need to find the right person to share my life with and yet so far, I got nothing. Should I give up on looking and pursue something else that would give me the satisfaction that I lack in that department? Maybe I should just accept the reality that I will live and die in this world a lonely person. Without a family to love and cherish, without anyone to hold on to, nevertheless, deep down, there is the feeling that pushes me to be with somebody, to belong and not just be a part of something you can throw away once their done passing it around. I am neither a piece of cloth that can be discarded when its filled with filth, nor a toy that can be easily put together once it's broken or damaged. I have feelings like everybody else, who is not immune to emotional attacks and lack of feelings.

But like a scene that's been played out many, many times over, I end up alone, again! Which is not surprising, somehow this has been a usual routine for me. I find someone I like, it could be anyone from all walks of life, and it really doesn't matter. Let's just say it's another fellow that I want to be friends with; I met him, got to know him a bit, and somehow befriended him. Then, we exchange numbers just to keep in touch. I call; we talk. He said he'll come over to my house to hang out; I wait, I call again, no one answers. I tried again for the second and third time, now its busy. I give a couple of hours to wait before I give it another try, and when it's almost time for me to hit the sack, I tried for the last time. It rings and somebody answered. It's him; I ask why he stood me up. Makes a bunch of excuses and finally I gave in. Fine with me, since I want to be his friend, I want him to like me and to get to know me.

The sequence is then repeated several more times during the course of a week, until he finally comes over, but not alone, he brought a friend along with him. Then, he'd ask me if I could do them a favor, I said yes, out of the kindness of my heart, so I did what he asked. Afterwards, he again ask me if I could give them a ride and drop them off at a friend's house, reluctantly I agreed with a sigh of frustration. I end up all by myself, again. I let them use me, again. I am alone, again!

Such a shame that a guy like me can't even get a decent person to share my life with, or just have somebody around when you need them. I've always longed for someone who share the same interest as I do, my likes and dislikes, that sort of thing, but we all know that this is next to impossible, unless, there's someone out there that looks, sounds, and behaves exactly like me down to the molecular level. Like a clone. Like the ones I see on movies and news lately, hmn, that would be great, except, why would I even consider that possibility. I mean, come on, another me, no way! I never did like me. I was ugly during my first twelve years in grade school. I was ugly in high school, in college, well at least, I got rid of the horrible acnes that were part of puberty, but I was still ugly. Add to the fact that I rarely have social skills. If you can call making people laugh in the expense of others a social skill, well I don't know what to say, except, that they're crazy. Nevertheless, that's what I often do to others, it seems cruel, but it's the only way I know. I only do it for reasons of wanting to be accepted, to make people like me, to make them see me pass my exterior vulnerabilities and imperfections, rather, to see as what I truly am. A nice guy with a loving and compassionate heart, one who likes to tell jokes to people and not make fun of them, but also would like them to know that as a person I hold their trust in my hands, and I would keep it firmly in my stead and I hope they would too. For there are secrets that need to be kept hidden and locked away in a closet until the person who carries such secret is ready and able to give consent. I have my own secrets to hide, secrets that I myself am afraid of telling or even divulging, for that matter. I have a secret. No one knows about it, except a very few friends of mine, friends that I grew up with and up until now been in constant contact with. They are my best friend, my confidants, people who have been there for me in times when I feel as if the world is against me and in many occasion, I've been there for them. Through our difficulties and triumphs, disappointments and regrets, we have each shared all these and more. We have formed a kinship unlike any other, a bond that can never be broken or challenged. That's why the friends I have are the ones I keep. They know what I know, and yet the secret that we try to keep from being disclose may also be the reason behind our constant mockery that's being thrown at our faces by 'intolerable people'.

We are all living a lie! From the moment we meet another person other than a family member, we try to out do the other by pretending to be better than they are. It's perfectly normal, in a way, since people do tend to pretend to be someone other than themselves. However, it's not the same with me, with us. My friends and I are very different from the rest of humanity, always in constant alert of others' reaction, being aware of everything and everybody, not knowing whom you can trust and whom you should stay away from. Will I be willing to trust them with my secret? Is it enough to know someone for a couple of years before you let them know what you really are? Such a hard task to carry, yet I the bear the burden of an enormous responsibility of being different, being someone I'm not.

Nevertheless, no matter how careful I can be, no matter how discreet I present myself, something always slips between the cracks and they know. Someone always wants and tries to piece together the puzzle of what makes us tick, of what makes me tick. And they know, or do they? These are the people that I look out for the most, whose intentions are not pure but of deception and intrigue, people who try to find out who and what I really am behind the façade that I have intricately created and protected.

Protecting it from guilt, embarrassment, and ultimately, the shame it might bring to myself and to the ones I love. So much confusion, so much anger inside of me, not knowing if they truly know, or knowing if they do know, what I am to them. I don't know; I am still…confused.

It's funny to think that no matter what I do, try to make sure that no one knows what I so desperately try to hold back in me, even going as far as to making a point to remind myself to act the way people expect me to act. Consciously being aware of how I present myself to others; every inch of every movement that

I make are carefully planned, thought of and finally, executed with enough manner that no one would suspect, but as I said, someone always does. Can I help it?

Maybe, if I could only tell them the truth, let them know who I really am, stripped of the façade and inhibition and finally releasing myself of the burden that has been haunting me since the day I realized that I am...a closet?

No, I am not ready! I can't even put it into words much less say it aloud for everyone to know. However, I think I have an idea that they know who they are so desperately trying to piece together. I won't even be surprise if they say that they knew it from the start, that their only keeping it to themselves for reasons of either not hurting my feelings or simply because of the fact that fear of embarrassment and shame they get from others just from the mere association from the likes of me. Such a shame that I have to resort to being someone I'm not, that I can't be who I really am, afraid that I will be mocked and scorned if they do find out.

Someday I will have the courage to let them know who I am, despite of what they think and in spite of all the consequences I may face on that day, I will still hold my head up high. But for now, I will keep this chapter on my life an open book, to sort out the confusions that hang over my head, to bring about solutions to my problems, and to be completely and utterly devoid of anger and frustrations, and in the end to finally be free!

8

A CRISIS WITHIN

Look at this mess. My room was never like this back home; shirts, socks, even underwear on the floor, on top of cabinets, everywhere. Too many things that are not in place and yet I haven't had the slightest idea where to begin. In fact, when I was growing up, it was never an excuse to leave your room in such a conspicuously disarrayed manner. Our mom would have our heads off, besides she taught us better than that. Just that sound of that word, mom, it gives anyone a heartfelt relief and comfort for anyone seeking love and affection. Hey, I may not like all this mushy stuff and the dramatics, but I'm beginning to realize the importance of what she had instilled in us; to be responsible in everything we do and accept the consequences that follow. I have learned that from her and I am now grateful that without her I couldn't do the things I want to.

Among the five sons she had, I was the one, who she constantly takes wherever she goes. It wasn't a choice on my part, I couldn't say no either since she was like a fire that can never be expunged once she had set her mind onto something, or you can never get away from her since she knows everything that we do. I guess it was her way of bonding with me by taking me to places where she needed my input. She dealt with us differently and according to her own terms, it worked in the long run in spite all the rebellions she had to encounter from each one of us. However, she influenced me in a different way, since I somehow acquired some of her characteristics, the mannerism, as well as the decision-making and the how I handle things. Is this a good thing? I don't know, in a way, I guess, since I manage to keep myself from ever getting into major trouble and disaster. But it also affected me in a way where I had to delude many people and myself included. When it comes to being around people, I have the social skill of what you call an outcast, always alone and nobody to talk to unless approached and spoken to. Other than that, I have pretty much given up on ever getting anybody to like me for who I am. Hey, I'm friendly, I'm nice, is there anything else I need to do to make them like me? Come to think of it, I mostly get those comments from girls. I never had a guy tell me I'm like that or like this, guys just don't do that, its part of our silent pact thing, you girls wouldn't understand it anyway. It's just that all I remember growing up was a bunch of girls hanging around me, playing and wanting to always be with me. I don't want to sound that I'm proud of it, I'm not, well...I kind of like it, nevertheless, whenever I want to hang with my own gender, it makes me feel different. Like it's not right. When I'm around them, I'm thinking, "What would people be saying about me being the person that I am?" Do they cringe, or would they applaud me? The truth is; I just wanted to talk, to hang out with them, nothing else. On the other hand, is it just that?

I know that I'm aware that being with them would only result into a major problem, and more confusion, especially on my part, but this is what I feel and it's a burden I have to carry for as long as I am able. There's not a day that goes by that I don't feel this way, and it's driving me insane. Is it a genetic thing? Better yet, a socially triggered situation or an environmentally influenced illness. I have no idea whatsoever. There are times that I don't even care anymore! To be a part of everyone is all I wanted, to share everything that I know and realize that what their looking at is a person that they can trust and be friends with. Which takes me to yet another part of my life that confuses me? Who am I? Moreover, what do I really want? To answer that, I have to divulge everything I know about myself, and that would take courage. Courage that I don't have right now, for I still have to iron some things out and it would probably take me forever before I can do anything. But other than what stands before you, I have nothing to hide, except, to be careful with what I do for there are vultures who try to devour whatever and any information concerning someone they dislike and someone they know is a threat to their very existence. My business is mine alone to deal with, and they need not concern themselves, until, of course, I am ready to impart with them what I know. Until that time comes, accept me for who I am, otherwise, it really doesn't matter.

9

RESOLUTION

A lot have been said and written about my father, all the anger that I have for him for not loving us the way our mom loves us. The fear that he instilled in our hearts in moments of mistakes and mishaps on our part, the constant nagging of how irresponsible his sons are, and how our mom have failed us the way he wanted his sons to be brought up.

All of these and more are done and buried, buried beneath tons of dirt and rocks where no one can dig it up if ever someone wants to bring up our past. A past that hopefully have been forgiven, but not completely forgotten, for only when you learn from your past can someone be truly forgiven. I have forgiven my father. The way he is, and the way he was like. It's hard to think that after all these years, after all the sufferings I have endured in the hands of the person who I longed to be with; I finally realize that I do have feelings for him.

Maybe, I'm reaching the pinnacle of emotional maturity. As I grow older, I have come to the conclusion that my father did his best in raising us in every way he can. He may not be the perfect father that most kids have, I mean, growing up he was there for us constantly, providing us with all our needs, both physically and emotionally. He also has taught us skills to survive in a world that's very different from the one he grew up in.

He was telling us how terrible his life was when he was growing up, that they never had all the basic things a person needs to get through the day. Nevertheless, they did, they have survived. All six of them and a mother who did everything she could to make sure that her children, three boys and three girls, would grow up to be somebody, to see that they have a future. Moreover, to make it possible for the next generations that they wouldn't experience and suffer what they have gone through. Their mother was everything to them, since their father had passed early on. She was both a pillar of courage and inspiration. From dusk 'til dawn, she was in constant move to provide for her little ones, she saved everything from empty cans of food to sacks of flour where she made them into toys and clothes that they can use and play with. She encouraged her children to stand up on their own, to let no one and anything be an obstacle to their success. She is a strong willed woman, who speaks her mind without thinking about the consequences of what she says to others, the effects that it might have to a love one. That's probably the reason why, we, her grandchildren, made a silent pact amongst ourselves to never cuss or utter foul words to anyone or to anybody; besides, it never really sounded good anyway. I'm glad to this day I've never heard such foul words coming from any of my brothers or cousins.

Just like my grandmother, my father was like her, he made sure we had everything from the food we eat, to the clothes we wear, to the toys we like to have. We got them all. He is a good provider, a good father. In the past, I have written things that would have hurt him, that would make any father weep. Not this time.

I won't write anything negative or bad about my father, for I have also learned from my mistakes, from my past. Maybe I never really did give him a chance to explain or understand what he was going through, what he went through. I've probably never live up to his expectations both as a son and as a man. Being his son, I should have been there for him, supported him, help him to whatever way I can. Not giving him more problems, not always getting into little troubles, I should have behaved in a manner I was taught. And when I grew older, I realized that there are more to life than what I have thought it to be. I often screw up and make mistakes that would define me as a man, and when I did, I turn to my father for support, a net to catch me when I fall atop a so-called pedestal where I egotistically placed myself onto. I've never met any challenges headstrong. That's probably the reason why I failed him as man. A man should be able to face adversities by himself, to be as strong as his father was. I failed many times; I realize it was already too late.

However, the one of the many things I've learned from my father is to persevere in times when everything may not look so bright, to remember that there's always a way out to every difficulty, to be strong and not be discourage.

This is the legacy that he will leave behind. His children finally coming into terms and realizes that no matter what they do, that no matter where they go, he will always be with us, with me, in my heart. Passing it to my children and to my children's children as well, the love that he gave and the sacrifices he endured will always be in me. For he love us so dearly that he gave us all that he had and more.

And because of this, I truly can say that I LOVE MY DAD!

10

LOVE THEM, HATE THEM

I envy them. Those people whose lives are so different from mine, sometimes I'd tell myself that I'm missing so much in life, all the wonderful things that I could do if only I were somebody other than my own. Places I could go if I were born on a different setting in a different family, or being somebody who knows that he can do things that only a handful of people can do.

It's amazing to see people, kids in particular, with enormous talents; dancing, singing, creating, performing, doing the things they are born to do and still having so much fun as well as recognition both from their peers and from their admirers. Have I missed so much in life that every time I see somebody like them I feel jealous? No, not so much as jealousy since I don't think that this emotion particularly fits the description, but rather, having the feelings of thrill, excitement, wonderment and most of all, envy. Compared to them, I'm almost at the prime of my life. Being in my twenty's and not having accomplish anything worthwhile, would definitely make me feel less of a person, a person whose destiny I'm not quite sure of. Do I have what it takes to be somebody in this world we live in? Probably, but unless I do something about it, I will remain this forsaken individual whose existence lies in my hands and the quality of life I lead. But right now, at this very moment I feel disappointed, angry and ashamed of myself, not for having been born famous or rich, nor having the courage to overcome adversities and defeats, rather, not having all the talents and the God-given gifts to share it with others and for others to see and admire, and to achieve such recognition at an earlier age. How I wish that I could do those things that one as talented as they could do. Is it too late for me to accomplish this? I think so, I wonder then, what would it be like if I were one of them; to see what they see, to know what they know and having the awareness of myself, the consciousness I have right now being what I am, incorporated into their young talented personalities. Moreover, retaining the memories I have when I was what I am. It's rather

28

difficult to explain this, yet this is what as far as I can tell; I want to be one of them, be a young, good-looking boy with talents to back me up.

This is what I've always wanted ever since I became aware of myself looking at a young boy's features, a Caucasian boy for that matter. It wasn't something that I chose to do, nor it was an attraction that many might misinterpret, simply, a moment where I have never experienced something like this at first hand, to realize that I am different. Moreover, someone out there could be better than who I am. Soon the feeling of envy envelops me, to know that I could never be like them. They have so much going on for them, physical features of perfection; a nice smooth legs with muscles undeveloped yet shows a promising future, a body that rival's any averaged muscled man, who longs to create a body devoid of fat, and a face, what can I say. Those wonderful big beautifully colored eyes and their perfectly shaped brows that shows so much emotions; lips that speaks volumes even without uttering a single word. It draws me near it, to touch, to taste, and even kiss and caress such object. On the side of their face, and on their arms and legs, tiny beautiful baby blond hairs that glisten whenever the sun flashes its rays on them, and those feet; different shapes and sizes, they have so much magnetism that draws me into them, longing to have a pair as nice and as beautiful as they have. Only to awaken from a deep slumber that what I am is neither a perception of what I thought I was nor a belief that I am somebody I'm not. Despite all that, it still try to be one of them, to be like them, thinking and somehow acting like them in a manner that would not compromise my own self, looking like an idiot of some sort. Being a kid in a grown man's body, crazy as it may sound, I've always have the feeling that I'm supposed to be someone other than me. I never liked my own body as far as I can remember; I shied away from ever letting myself look in the mirror. Knowing I possess grotesque features that nobody would dare want; a face that have no shape nor form, a pair of legs that looks like a baseball bat…no, actually a stick, with no muscles, no shape, no promise that will bring a brighter tomorrow, rejected by many, ashamed to even think that I have something to be proud of.

These are the situations that I have to live with every single day, things where I feel regret because of what has been handed down to me, of how I turned out to be. Yes, I do feel some regret having been born like this, a person of average features and characteristics that could not set me apart from others, things that would make me realize that I do have the physicality of someone special, where people would admire and like to be. Having the charisma and the innocence of a child and possessing the physical features of a teen-age white boy.

Would it be nice to be them, boys of their kind well endowed and at that age? I would love being like them, to be a kid again. If I could only just put myself, the mind that I have right now, into theirs, replacing what they have and integrating my own into their mind and body, constantly knowing and experiencing that I'm in the body of a young Caucasian boy who has the looks and body that I longed for. To be desired and admired, to be envied by many, and be able to look at myself in the mirror without hesitation and regret that for once and, maybe forever, that I am satisfied…happy with what I am and possess. Selfish, I think not. If only I can explain the way that I'm feeling, maybe, people would understand, maybe they would not judge me so much. However, this is how reality controls people, like me, I have desires and frustrations, ambitions and failures. Even though, being somebody I'm not is what I crave for and for all the advance and modern breakthroughs that anyone can accomplish nowadays, I will remain the same person born on this world, full of emotions brewing inside, emotions that may sprung up anytime and anywhere, by anyone or anything. I will always put everything into words to vent and express feelings I have, good or bad.

This is what I do best, and I'm not ashamed of it.

11

GIFTED

I am a dreamer. I have been since at a very young age, I still remember the times I've spent in my room or anywhere else of my choosing, that I dream of myself being somebody else, far apart from what I used to be. The things I can do if I were somebody strong, who can do things that anyone and everyone would be awe struck by the immense strength I possess. Then there are days that I dream of myself performing on a stage full of spectators eager to watch me execute, act and display certain movements that I alone can do but not impossible for others to perform, yet with me performing such acts, I have raised the standards of how future competition would be based upon. I am an athlete, one that is admired and adored by all. And on other occasions, I am what other people might envy, having been blessed with features that sets me apart from others. Giving me an advantage to promote myself and my image on magazine covers or television shows, or even having my body covered only by a piece of cloth that I'm promoting posted on a billboard somewhere along the fashion walls at the heart of New York. People staring, looking and admiring my face, my body well defined as though created from clay into a perfect David.

This is the part I like the most, the part where girls swoon over my looks and wants me all for their own. Where guys want to be like me, not for having the perfectly chiseled body, rather, for having all the girls desire you, to love you, so many things that I could do if I only were that person I'm dreaming of, the admiration that I could get, the adulation from others that I may possess. In addition, to finally feel that you have something that I could be satisfied with, that I alone have and possess. I dream…then reality sets in. I am back. To a world where I am but a regular guy whose looks may not be as desirable as one would admire, nor possess talents and God-given gifts that could make me famous or rich. These are the things that make me wonder if I ever do have a purpose in life. Am I destined to become someone talented and gifted? Enough to be recognized and remembered for the contributions that I have given to the people, or simply another forgotten face in the crowd, not to be remembered, nor accepted. Just a piece of washcloth that's easily discarded once it has served its purpose.

No! I will not let this happen. Not to me, I will not allow it.

Each passing day that comes and go, I am reminded of things that in the long run, I will be remembered by some, if not all, for the works that I've done and will do. However it may appear, grand or small. It will always bear my mark, leaving behind printed words or silhouette of lights and shadows that would remind them that once there was a person who had the potential of greatness and still had the courage to not be ashamed of being emotional.

Indeed, there are so many things that need to be discovered and seen in so many different directions, that one may not suspect its right under their noses. Talents and gifts that once lay dormant are now willing to expand its horizon and to eventually flourish in its newfound glory. Such is not impossible to phantom, they only need is to look inside of themselves and they might be surprised with what they see. God has been kind to me, for He has shown me that I have the gifts of writing and artistry. Gifts that I've never known I had, had I not been so interested in things so different, things that are so opposite from my own. Where reality stops and fantasy begins, a place where imagination runs rampant and no limits to every desire you can mutter. I dream day in and day out, almost constantly, giving myself some needed relief to the ever-growing mischief and heartaches the world may offer. Although, temporary the solution that it may give, it has given me the chance to improve myself in terms of artwork and literary pieces; paintings, essays, poems, countless pieces that I've created. Simple works of art that have turned into something I would never have dreamed of, that all these came from by just holding a piece of paint brush and letting my fingers do the filling. Blanks of canvases that has been transformed into colorful artworks where fantasy meets reality and where reality may not appear as someone may perceive it; or having a piece of paper be filled with written words that expresses so much feelings, so much emotions that sometimes it surprises me that all this came from me.

Words, at first, may not mean anything, but once it begins to share its simple letters and syllables to form a simple phrase that expresses something you feel inside, it will then be realized that what I have been trying to impart and share. A sense of knowing that someone else out there other than me, even if it means that there's only one person in the crowd amongst many, is having and experiencing the same exact emotions I'm having in a particular situation I'm in. Then I am relieved to know that I'm not the only one, I'm not alone in the universe. Some-one out there understand what I'm going through, that in a way we share a life that is not so different from each other. Bringing ourselves together, if not closer, to events that made us what we are. Experiences that have shaped our path and to continue building and re-building ourselves, myself, into something that makes me stronger than I was before.

This is the power and the glory of what writing can give me, the freedom to know that I can scribble down anything I feel no matter what the outcome it might bring. To realize that I have given someone something special to treasure and reminisce about of what it was like when one such as me lived his life, my life. To them it is like a journey through my eyes, to see what I've seen where people react and show what they really are. To see the things that made me writhe and shudder in moments of lust at first sight, to know what true love really feels like, through my eyes, the moment you see the right person, your soul mate, then and only then that you know. Moreover, through the words that I have written, it will take them into boundless, endless sights and imaginations of what I went through as a boy and as a man who became what he is and what he was, just by being true to himself, and still remaining as somewhat secretive and mys-terious all at the same time.

My works, my creations, my masterpieces will indeed survive the passage of time, forever instilling and sharing in the hearts of any curious minds of how I lived my life, overcome adversities and inspire to create works of art and literary pieces that have meant so much to me.

Telling each a story of how, when, why, and to whom it was created. More-over, to finally leave behind a legacy that someday it will be criticized, studied, argued about and accepted not for its infamous words or highfalutin phrases, but rather on its simplicity, originality, and the desire to be heard and felt no matter how insignificant it may seem. Although, opinions are notable, in the end it is never needed, for one's own is enough, to be true, to be me.

12

PILLAR OF FIRE

Sometimes it takes the right person to mold someone in to the person they will one day turn out to be. Someone they could be proud of, someone they can shape and teach on how to cope and survive in a world full of regrets, frustrations and misinterpretations. A person who helps you on how to adapt to whatever challenges that fate brings, to face life head on and be not afraid if failure comes for it will only make you stronger and learn from it. Don't let vulnerability be a sign of weakness, but to see it as something different where you let yourself be felt and acknowledged by everyone around you. To accomplish a goal that may have been difficult to reach is always something to feel good about, and if anything ever goes wrong, always remember that someone, a special person, will forever be there to lend you a hand. To help you get through a task that maybe difficult for someone like you to deal with, where there's so much confusion and lack of resources that at times giving up is the best way to let yourself out. Someone who has become an unending presence to guide you in your darkest hour, to see the light no matter how faint and bleak, reminding you that there is a way out in a tunnel full of endless darkness. Just listen to your heart enough to remember and know that there's a way to alleviate yourself of all the chaos that baffles your soul. Reach out and fill yourself with the love that she has provided and maybe more, more than you know; A breath of life, a love that is unending, a fire that cannot be expunged, moreover, a name that we always call out in times of despair and comfort; Mother, Mommy, Mama.

To me she's just Mom, but of course, she is more than that and not only an ordinary mom. She has filled many shoes, became different persons in times when she feels that her sons are troubled by the demands the world may ask of us. She's been a figure that has become a symbol of light in our struggle to become who we are, constantly making herself the guiding presence in our everyday life. Making sure that the decisions we make and the paths we take are the ones that would make us happy and satisfied. In her mind, she has already planned what her sons would be like, yet she never pushed nor stirred us to a path that we never would want, a path that would certainly make her happy and proud on how we turned out. But rather, she gave us enough advice to make our own decisions and even though, we may never pursue something that she feels that it's our best chance of surviving, a chance that would make each one of us grow into our predetermined future. A future pre-conceived in every minds and hearts of every parent out there. She has and will always be proud of us no matter how we turn out.

Raising kids is a job that requires a lot of work that does not only involve providing basic needs and believing that everything will be pleasant and cheerful once a need is satisfied. Rather, molding a person's character through teaching and letting them know that consequences are abound in times when decisions are made hastily and without much thought. To show them rewards that they can reap once they have achieve a task they longed to acquire, and to show them that love is unconditional no matter how we make out with our lives. It's hard to imagine that one person can do all these and still be an inspiration to others. My life may not have turned out as others might expected, where all my dreams and aspirations have been fulfilled, or problems and hardships are easily solved and where everybody comes into terms as though nothing can deter them from anything or anyone. Who wouldn't want to have a life like that? Why can't it happen to anyone? Why doesn't it happen at all? But then again, if you think about it, who would want it, would anyone be happy with the life they have if everything they want and wish for falls into place, even though it was gained from nothing? Where hard work and perseverance were not a part of the one thing they wanted the most, and that is, to grow and achieve into what we desire for in life, and is usually attained through how we face life's ever-changing expectations from us. Each of us is given a choice on how we live our life, and a chance to live through our misguided directions either to learn from it, or to stay away from ever getting involved in the same situation. Second chances are a few and limited to certain people, that's why we need to grasp every opportunity, every moment that we have to let ourselves be an instrument of learning and let certain sacrifices be made in order for us to flourish into whatever goal we set our sight into.

I'm still learning and for that matter, surviving in this world, where one can suffocate with just the overcrowding of people trying to make it big in a place where there are fewer opportunities than there are people. Fewer still are the ones where their achievements are recognized. One might be considered lucky if their contributions and achievements to the world are recognized and remembered by others, yet it sometimes come at a great price. Where they can no longer appreciate the works they have done and enjoy the fruits of their labor, for times have passed and they are but a distant memory, only their works are what's left of them. No one to explain nor reason out the works they have created, no one to question them and give out their answers, and most of all, no one to let us know the person behind their achievements. The force that has made them who they are, to have reach such heights that only a handful have accomplished and still are humbled by what they have been taught and learned through their constant interactions with their mothers. An inspiration indeed, if you look at the greatest works of the artists of our time, they have somewhat, if not totally, based their great works of art through the women that have shaped their lives; Mona Lisa, Madonna and child, and even the women characters in Shakespeare's numerous plays. They have each inspired them to create something that they all have adored and respected, moreover, loved, their mothers. If only we could ask what truly inspired them to create such masterpiece, if only they were here to share everything they know about how they lived, yet we'll never know. However, I know for a fact, that they would unanimously tell us that they were inspired by their mothers to be the best in everything they do, and doing such works of art are just a simple way of saying to their mothers, 'I love you.'

My way of telling my wonderful mom that I love her may not be as simple as saying the words, for she has done so much for me that she deserves better and more. One that she would treasure forever and for others to know and realize that if it wasn't for the love she gave me and the lessons she instilled in my heart, I would never have achieve a life that are full of comfort and challenges. The life I have right at this moment may not be perfect, where there are too many problems and frustrations I've encountered; some end in defeat, while others, triumphant. I might have said and done things that I'm not proud of, things that have hurt people and maybe scarred them for life. In spite all that, I wouldn't take back anything that have had happened to me. For it is what defines me as a person raised by my mom, who emanates integrity, well-being and so much life for her children, that she treated her role not as a job or duty, nor obligation for a mother to perform. But of love and respect for the gifts she had received, moreover, to shape their lives into the best of her capabilities. Each of us owes a lot from our mother, and it is at this very moment that I dedicate my life and the countless works I've made to the one person that have inspired me to strive my best in everything that I do. To give it all my worth and to share it with others, the love that she gave me, the life she had given me. Truly, a blessing to have a person like her in my life, who has touched my heart and in the end, she will always be with me. She gave me my life, she prayed for my soul, and in return, I will forever be in debt and grateful for the things she had done and sacrificed. For that matter, she is truly a love incarnate.

I love you mom; this is for you.

13

AS I WALK THROUGH THE VALLEY OF...

✦

DEATH.

A subject that brings fear to the eyes of everyone, to know that when there's a beginning, there has to have an end. And death is the final chapter to everyone's life.

No matter how much we try to cheat death, to manipulate physical barriers by making ourselves look younger and stronger, or concocting numerous technological discoveries and advances that would give us our youth, forever trying to give ourselves the ultimate gift; immortality. Anything to deter the force that would take us away from the place we are grounded to a world where none of us knows. Death is indeed the end. No one knows exactly where we go when our life shuts down and we can no longer be a part of the living, when the time comes that families have to say their goodbyes and farewells.

Sometimes we never get to have that chance, to say how we feel to a loved one when its time for them to move on…move on to where? People say to each other, especially to their children, when a love one died, that they're now in a better place where they're much happier. Where there's no pain or suffering, hate or diseases. A place full of love and affection, a paradise, it's the term people use to describe a perfect place where they want to be at, either to live in or it becomes a place in their hearts to give them comfort and ease when its time for them to leave the land of mortals. Believing that death is another step towards salvation, moreover towards ultimate evolution, this is our way of telling ourselves that we're going to a better place. Creating an idea that there is really a place out there for us, making ourselves believe in the fact of such place behind a so-called truth. A fairytale, a fantasy? I don't know.

Nevertheless, no matter how much we try to dissuade ourselves of the fact that maybe, just maybe, there's nothing for us out there, just emptiness, not even a conscious thought, or an awareness of one's own existence. Absolutely nothing at all. What lies ahead after our brief encounter in this world would definitely scare anyone. I, too, am scared, afraid of not knowing what will happen to me after death. Dying itself is only a process that will bring you towards the end, but to experience the magnitude and power of death itself is something that keeps me awake at night. I'm afraid to die, not knowing if there's a place for me out there; a Heaven, a hell, or anything that will tell you that you still exist, but in a rather different persona, anything that will tell me that, 'you are here, and you need not be afraid.' However, if there were indeed such a place, would there be anyone to greet us, to show us around, to love us and embrace our essence? I really have no way of knowing what's out there, and I am not looking forward to it.

Every time I think about the years that will come, the years that I still have, ten, twenty, or thirty years from now, I say to myself, will I still be here. To experience the things to come and the moments I'm still destined to experience, and be involved in anything that would keep me going, that will make me realize that I'm still alive.

I'm afraid that all the things that I've learned, the things I've been taught to believe in; our faith, our savior, our God, were all a façade of our unending fear of death. That when we first learned of the death concept and its impact on our society, its implications that there may not be anything at all for us out there, we simply resorted to our inner childhood, repressed anything that would give us fear. Thus, created a persona in the form of a higher Being that would serve both as a comfort to us and ultimately becomes our goal to be with on the day of our demise, that all faith, all religion are/was based on this concept of a higher power. A God and its reason for its creation was our extreme fear of death.

Why can't we live forever? Better yet, why do we have to grow old? Growing old comes the fact that you are nearing the end of your journey. A journey wherein you may not be ready to give up and hand it over to somebody you believe in, only because this is what it's supposed to be. A destiny passed down from generations to generations to realize that after life, death is the end. The subject of death truly gives me something to think about, and it scares the hell out of me! I don't know how to neither end nor begin to explain what I'm feeling or how to start and finish the topic or even give any reason or simple explanation just to ease my fear. The anxiety that overwhelms me every time I think about what would happen to me after my life has ended. Nothing seems to work, no one to turn to, for comfort and understanding. Nonetheless, after all the things that I have thought about, the explanation and reasons for our fear, the creation of an excuse to soothe our anxiety and to eventually comfort our soul. It is to the one Being, the Higher Power that I turn to, not because there's no one else to go to, nor it's the last resort I can think of. Rather, it's a feeling that brings you back to where you belong, that somehow, somewhere inside of you, there's a force that tells you the answer is simple, and its right where you least expect it to be. It's a place you call home, a Father that is waiting to welcome you back with open arms and grandiose. That in our need to find things that are of interest to us, to explore new discoveries and surroundings, constantly being curious to all things unnatural and natural, we sometimes end up looking back and not finding the path that would lead us back to our home.

Regrets have been plenty, sins have been committed, yet through it all, He has always provided us with a beacon to light our path that will take us back to Him. To His loving arms, whose heart is pure and whose forgiveness is limitless. No matter how much I try to reason out any explanation to what I may have when I die, or the overwhelming fear that surrounds me, it is through His love that gives me comfort and joy. Knowing one day, I will soon be joining Him, to celebrate my return, to meet my families, and to realize that finally, I am home.

14

IN HIS LIKENESS

From the depths of the unknown, to the surface that is of this world, out comes a person. He cried out for no reason, may it be from the stress and pain of getting pushed out of the one place you called home for the past lifetime, or may be from the moment you realized that you are no longer a part of a whole. To be no longer dependent from the mother who has taken care of you. You who have shared her breath, to let her know that you are in need of nourishment, to let someone touch you through your mother's love, however, this time the bond that binds you together has been severed from its core. You came out not knowing what to expect, silence fills the room, then you feel a slap from behind and you cried. Pain rushed your body liked you've never felt before, you see the world so differently, so out of focused, then you take your first breath and you cried out. For once, you will no longer be a part of her, to be on your own, and that scared you. So you cried, and cried until she held you in her loving arms and whispered comforting words to your ear, to let you know that she's still here to help you be who you want to be. Then, you eased up and stopped crying, realizing that you are her life, how you meant so much to her, how you made her so happy. She cries, not for the pain she endured nor the long hours spent waiting for the moment to come, but for the happiness it brought her when the fruit of her labor has finally arrived. A gift from above, a newborn, a neophyte on this world, it both excites and overwhelms her from the sheer presence that you bring to this world. From that moment, she realizes to make sure that nurturing you is her foremost priority, to bring you up the way you are destined to be, then, she utters the word that would describe you for the rest of your life. She whispers, as if receiving it from heaven, your name for the very first time…Melvin.

Yeah, it's me! It's my chance to reveal how I came to be in this world we call home, although, I've not quite mastered the art form of having my life bear open for everyone to scrutinize, I will take it as it is, with open mind and subject to criticisms. For what is life without obstacles and the chance to find out what I was really like as a child? To know the people behind my success and failures, as well as role models, and to look what lies ahead beyond the obvious, and who better tell it but yours truly.

As a child, one of the things I remember when I was back home was the fact that I had many girlfriends, not the type where you cuddle and kiss, or whatever things a couple do, rather girls I mostly played with. I like playing with them and almost most of the time they like playing with me, maybe since I never had a sister to play with, or they never had a brother to boss them around, either way, we did play together. My older brother, on the other hand, is different; he and I were about four years apart. He had his first four years of his life before I entered his; he had everything he wanted, from the toys he likes to the love of parents as well as admiration from other relatives. That's probably why he can easily cope to his surroundings, even though things may not go so well for him. I don't even remember the times when he got jealous of me, from the things I had and given to me, he's so composed and sure of himself that he had a lot of friends. From our own neighborhood to his school campus and he love girls, so much so that he always had a different girl come over our house every night either to chat or to study with them. But I'm pretty sure that's not all his after, since most girls I meet throw themselves at him at a moments notice.

He rarely plays with me, and I understood that, so I let him do his own thing, and I, on the other hand, play with our neighborhood girls. We played a lot of games, but mostly I remember playing with is the popular jump rope. It's a game where two people hold a piece of rope at each end and the other player would try to jump over the rope, which goes higher, and higher 'til that person can't jump over it anymore. Then each player take their turns, I have long legs, so I often win. It's kind of fun in a way, since I never liked rough games. I don't like to get hurt, much, so I preferred back then to play with them, which in retrospect, is the reason of my downfall. You see, people started to notice that I hang with girls almost all the time, and doing things that a typical boy don't normally do, they started asking questions, started to be curious about who I am and what I might become. Sometimes even throwing awkward looks in their eyes whenever I walk pass them, then you hear whispers between them, prompting me to think and ask myself, that you've somewhat made a habit of whenever someone like them are around. Are they talking about me? Are they saying things behind my back? You then wonder, and when I turn around and look at them, they suddenly stop talking and give me a smile, which quickly turn into burst of laughter. Yep, they definitely are talking about me.

Who the hell cares what they say anyway! Their just a bunch of old crows who likes to hang around street corners and drink beer and smoke cigarettes, they have neither jobs nor things to do, except be a menace to our society, just a group of freaks that nobody wants. I tried to ignore their taunts, thinking their no better than me, all I have to do is to make sure that I don't end up like them. In spite all that, it still didn't stop me from doing what comes naturally, that is, to play and have fun, no matter whom I play with. I enjoy girls' company, although, I kind of feel somewhat remorseful when at times I beat them at their games, the sad part is, when they lose, they like to tease me. I've been called many names by them, so instead of giving them a taste of their own medicine, I just went home. I left them whining their hearts out, and after that, they think that what I did was an act of cowardness, that I'm a chicken. I am not! I'd rather stay away from such violent out burst and immature tantrums that they so perfectly mastered, besides who would want to leave a fight bruised and worse debilitated. Not me, I'll leave all that to my brothers.

However, I wonder if the things I did when I was a child were just mere expression of what I will someday be judge upon, to one day realize that the mistakes I've made in the past are the ones that'll haunt me for the rest of my life. Some days, I question myself about how my life have turned out the way they have. Should I have done it differently? Am I willing to let it go and not allow any distractions to interfere with whatever outcome I may have? Maybe I should have thought about it with more seriousness and not let my easy-going, happy-go-lucky attitude take over the decisions that will one day affect my life. I've allowed my defenses to go disarray and the consequences of such actions have made an absolute affect on my lifestyle and the way I see things from a perspective of somebody who was supposedly destined to be a person that emanates qualities that would have been an envy of many. Instead, I have become someone who takes life as easily as taking a candy from a baby's hand. Never mindful about the feelings of others and what I others might think of me, always believing that everything will turn out the way it should. But it never does, I wasn't aware back then that life gives us ever-changing challenges that will eventually shape our lives. The way we're destined to become, and the way we make adjustments to events that'll lead to our destiny. Making sacrifices along the way and doing the best we can in everything we do, and hoping that the decisions we make are the ones that would lead to our salvation.

Looking back, I've realize that I never did any of those things. I would have done it differently have I been given a second chance in life, to change something not because it never turned out the way I expected it to be, but rather, to come to a more acceptable outcome now that I know things which I never knew back then. Maybe if I have done it the way I should have, the results would've probably been very different, maybe I would see things differently and somehow made the necessary changes if needed to, and I could have prevented something that would allow myself to be vulnerable to things that I would later regret in life. I still reminisce about the things I did when I was a child, and think about the changes I could have made. What if I can go back and tell my younger self that he needs to do things differently and put more thought into a situation before jumping into something that would surely put us in harms way.

Then again, if I ever did what would supposedly be my saving grace, maybe I wouldn't experience the things that have brought me profound changes in my life. I may never meet the people who would later be my confidants, or see the things I've seen if I were to give up being true to myself. Maybe I would not have the love and respect for my parents if I did everything on my own, my pride would have prevented me from doing the things I do with my parents, and I could never take that away. I just need to learn to accept my destiny whatever it may be, if I were to become nobody, so be it. There will be a time in my life, if lucky, after death that people will know my name and say that they knew me. A person of integrity and whose life, however I had lived it, has significantly affected theirs. That without me they would never have realized that being true to themselves and letting their emotions be an integral part of their being are something to be proud of, and would learn that the struggles and difficulties they encounter need not be faced alone. Together with the people they love, forever sharing a bond unlike any other will always come out standing tall, triumphant. Knowing that in the face of overwhelming darkness, they are not alone, someone will always be there to show them the way. My family has shown me the way time and time again, it is my fervent hope they realize that without them, I could never have lived my life to the fullest.

15

A LIFETIME AGO

High school was a time when people seemed so uncomplicated and at ease with their surroundings. Reveling in their own world, not minding that there are matters far more serious than what is portrayed inside their shielded home, where they can be easily eaten alive were they to venture outside the safe haven of their four-walled school. But that's what is good about being in high school, nothing to worry about except how you would look to your friends if they were to catch you in a very embarrassing and humiliating situation. A place where petty disputes are easily resolved and friendships may last a few weeks, while others, a lifetime. Nevertheless, for someone who is a neophyte removed from its protective bubble and thrown into the pack of hungry wolves, expecting it to survive and flourish, it was an experience so intimidating that getting up in the morning to go to school was as difficult as knowing that you will be alone once I stepped into that place. Nobody goes to my new school, 'cept one, but by the time we can rejuvenate our friendship, he would have gone to a different section and our paths would never cross again until graduation. This means I'm indeed alone in a place I know nothing of, where I am but one of many students trying to make sure that my day goes uneventful and untarnished.

While I may have stayed behind in own class and wallowed on my shortcomings, I met and befriended a fellow that would be a constant companion for me and would eventually share our everyday struggles and success, Christopher de Guzman was there for me and feisty he maybe sometimes, he was still a friend I can always count on. He introduced me to a world where I can use my imagination to my fullest potential, to see things where others might miss, and to believe in things that are out of the ordinary. A place in my mind where people have Marvel-ous powers and awesome abilities, where good fight evil, and where good people sometimes turn to the other side brought by the circumstances in their lives. Where things that are too unbearable and the only way for them to handle such difficulty is to choose a path they never have taken before. To go on the other side and experience what it's like to walk on the verge of darkness and evil, to give up everything that defines them a hero.

Sounds familiar isn't it; problems and struggles that a hero experience emulates to the problems and struggle that real people also experience. Art imitates life, in this case, comics' heroes and the situation their in, imitates the life of organics. To know that even powerful people have problems too, the capacity to fall apart when things seem so undeniably frustrating and confusing, I guess, that's the reason I can also relate to them. I have problems that may at times difficult to handle, but whenever I pick up a comic book and read the life of my favorite hero, I become that hero as well. To have the power and courage to do something about it, dramatically changing my personality to that of a hero I admire the most, and to wield the strength and stamina that no one has and that I solely possess. Moreover, showing others that they also have what it takes to beat the odds and arise triumphant, and to realize that behind the mask that their eager to conceal resides a person who experiences what any other person-hero or not-experience, theirs a hero in all of us, we may not have the abilities and powers that defines us heroes, what we have is far more sophisticated than that; will power. We've always had it and often times summons it to help us get through a tough situation, never realizing that it has saved us many times before.

This is one of the gifts that my friend, Christopher has given me, introducing me to a world of wonders and opening my imaginations where everything is possible even if it is only a make believe. His personality is another thing I like about him, we had so much fun together from the time we met in high school to our early years in college, and we did everything. We fight the fight that gives us the strength to overcome awkwardness during our years of considerable vicissitudes in school. We had the same out look in life and sometimes the people we like, and we go to places to have fun and get some needed relief from the overcrowding of home works that our teachers seemed so oblivious about. He was my companion and a confidant. We were like two peas in a pod, saying things what the other is thinking, even though we were thirteen back then, it was as if we knew each other longer and better than anybody else around did. I was proud to be his friend and we would do anything for each other, except one that is, I'm sure we both agree on this…You see, I later found out that what my friends and I have in common is the one thing that we try to conceal from others, especially to our close knit family, since it will only cause more confusion and distraught. So we just hide behind the walls of our school for protection, knowing it was the least of our problems, besides we were at a stage where discovering who we are, is as important as making our presence felt by everyone at school. After all, it's a popularity contest back then, and every move that anyone make, is noticed by everyone and that my friend, is what defines you as someone to be envied by everyone or someone who would always be seen walking alone along the hallways, never liked and remembered. However, my friends and I have somewhat left a mark in that place that somehow made us both adored and mocked by everyone. We know what we are and yet we were not afraid to show it to them and through this in your face attitude has what made us more of a target of mockery and dislike than acceptance. We had jocks, cheerleaders, freaks and geeks, and others you have no idea where they belong, but us, it's quite painfully obvious that we belong to the eccentric, the bizarre and outgoing type of people who just like to have fun. We are also smart, shy, aloft, strong willed and outspoken, qualities that anyone of these group can possess, yet ours is scorned and often times teased at by the majority of students just for being too different. Situations wherein we get emotionally drained from their constant cruelty, although, we hardly get into physical bouts with them, afraid that either one of us might be suspended or worse expelled, nevertheless, we are an unsuspecting target to their unyielding behavior. Only through our togetherness that we find a sense of safety and relief, and at times courage to let them have what they deserve by giving them their own medicine, since it's the only way for them to know how it feels like being on the receiving end. It rather gives us a moment to bask in our glory, but as always it never last, for there are many of them and only a few of us, and those who are like us are afraid to stand up for themselves and join our crusade. I couldn't blame them even if I wanted to, I surely didn't want it back then, but this is what the cards I'm dealing with; teased, scorned, hated by almost everyone.

This ongoing process would last four years, years of struggle and torment that would eventually turn into tolerance and acceptance. In due course, we each learned to accept the other, some might even say that we have grown so close that you couldn't tell one from the other. In fact, I was once considered an athlete, one of the best volleyball players in high school. I was already tall and lanky back then, qualities that they were looking for in a guy to play in a team, so I went in for the try out and fortunately for me I got in, so is Christopher, which made me even more happy since I have somebody I know to hang out with. We always were picked first in every game since we were the best, especially the time when we were up against a class that was a year ahead of us. They have this midget for a captain from which I was told has a mean streak of a spike pass. I wasn't really paying attention on his passes, rather on his large pimple on his nose; nevertheless, against someone like me, he was no match. Hitting him twice in the face by a ball sent by me, who I think he was trying to block my pass as I hit the ball over the net, and instead of hitting his hands, unintentionally, the ball found its way to his face. Thank God, his pimple was alright, besides it was redder than it was before, and his eyes were a little watery from the pain I somehow inflicted. Anyway, we won the match and headed to another game, unfortunately, we weren't able to advance to the finals as it was not meant to be, but the experience was well worth it. It was an amazing feeling, for a brief moment I was one of the guys, to belong to a regular group and got to know by everyone not only for my athletic prowess but also for my charismatic personality. I'm a funny guy, and people find my company to be exciting and comfortable, where they can feel at ease and are themselves. I got to know a lot of them; some even have become friends of mine, friends that I've been constantly with since the first day. Two of them eventually became more than just friends, for we have experienced and shared a life that somewhat mimics the other. We have become to each other a confidant and a brother through our unending struggle to find ways in dealing with our everyday demanding high school life, moreover, to move beyond simple reasoning and pursue the bigger picture, that we might learn the purpose of our being and to have something to contribute to the world we live in. Hoping that the works we leave behind will be enough for others to learn and know how we had the time of our life during our years in high school, that a typical boy like me can have a tremendous effect on others like them.

Four years of high school, years of struggle and fear that I may not fit in, yearning to belong and accepted by others, have all turned into memories that forever I will treasure. For without these, I wouldn't have met my friends, and the struggles that we've overcome together wouldn't have made each of us stronger and better than we previously were. I admire and love them like my own family, and even though I may not see them quite often since the distance between us is tremendously far from each other, wherein I'm living my life and so as theirs, we still share the same interests and aspirations now as we did back then. Still trying our best that our lives would end up the way we envisioned it, keeping in touch and hoping that someday we'll see each other again, soon I hope.

16

VILLAREAL

At first glance, I would not even give this guy a moment of my attention. I don't know him and neither does he know me, and yet, as I introduced myself to the person who would one day play a significant part in my life, only then I realized that I had nothing to worry about. Through our struggles in determining who we are and how our lives would unfold as we continue to lead the life, we are yet not completely familiar with, and in breaking barriers that was once considered forbidden from the likes of us. It was only through the bond we shared that we were able to conquer goals that would surely topple anyone, Conrad V., is definitely a friend I can count on. However, he's not the only one, I have one more friend that I put my trust into, and his turn will come eventually.

I was somewhat reluctant in getting to know him; he had a distinct presence that tells me that he may be hiding something far more than meets the eye. Giving some signs that he may well be what I think he is, yet, I was careful enough not to give away my own signals that I know what he might be hiding beneath that mask of deception. He has a sense of shyness and awkwardness that immediately gave him away. I, too, may have done the same thing, and he may have caught on to my own deception as well, nevertheless, we just let it go and moved on to our usual routine of conversing with other players during our gym class. Which is by the way, I was very much aware of, especially the players in our team. We had talented athletes that anyone would admire and would wish to emulate, for back then and until now, jocks have magnetism and a hidden charisma that makes them unique from everyone, drawing others into their own flock as though forming a barrier around them, protecting and making sure that no one claims their territory. There's a particular teammate I would want to emulate and protect, but it was something I didn't pursue since it was somewhere along the boundary of forbidden and insanity. I was not aware of it back then, but in the coming years of our high school life, that person will play a significant part in my coming of age and will forever be remembered and etched in my mind and my heart.

Anyway, as years pass by, Conrad and I have forged a kinship unlike any other, we understood what the other person is going through, even the people that give us inspiration to strive our best. If he favors a particular person that I know is rather difficult for someone like him to achieve, probably getting embarrassed for not having the courage to approach and deal with a situation that will surely put him in a tremendously awkward yet highly opportune moment. Nevertheless, it is an opportunity that I could never let it pass idle by, especially, when it comes to somebody he loves. Plans and favors have been set, leading to the moment that he'll be able to express feelings that I'm sure he has never quite experienced before. Though words seemed lacking for the moment when faced with a heavenly creature in front of him, I uttered the words that he wanted to express in his stead, words of comfort and compliment that made his love smile from ear to ear, a smile that melted away shyness and discomfort, eventually the wall that seemed so ever present in the eyes of my friend, preventing him from attaining a goal that for him has always been considered unreachable. Thinking that his unworthy of such divine presence, believing that one such creature of perfection could never be claimed nor possess by someone like him, whose spirit has been tormented by years of self-doubt and pity by who he is and what would become of him. All of it was swept away, leaving behind a person full of courage and awareness of himself and his surroundings, that he was finally able to perform the simplest thing in the eyes of his love: to say hello, and to be able to hear that same word reach his ear and pierce his heart, sweeping him off his feet. For a moment, he was complete, standing in the presence of perfection. It was enough for him even it was only for a fleeting moment, and it made him feel good inside. More words were uttered between them, watching them was something I will never forget, for it was as though they were meant for each other, no inhibitions whatsoever, and I could see it in his eyes that he was very much happy with what has transpired. The smile in his face was enough for me to know that he had liked what I did for him; no words needed to say how he felt, for I know exactly how he must be feeling. He would do the same for me, the bond we shared are so strong that we each know what the other person is going through and if one of us gets in to a situation we are too reluctant to pursue, one will certainly let himself on hand to help and lift up your spirit. Knowing that there will always be someone there when things you cherish may seem so uncertain, to give you advise on matters of the heart, and always valuing each other's opinion even when both are in disagreement.

Conrad is indeed a friend that can never be replaced, his been there for me through my difficult times when I have no way of knowing what would become of me if I ever pursue something that I considered unfamiliar and uncharted. He was there when he helped me accomplish tasks that I alone could not attain during my formative years in high school, he was an ever present figure if only in spirit the time I was in college when I was struggling to be someone I'm not. Concealing something I considered a flaw in my character, knowing that no matter how much I've changed in the years we've spent not seeing each other, he will always remember the real person in me. Reminiscing the times we've spent together from our teenage years, through our happy days in high school and during our much anticipated trials and tribulations in college. Moreover, through the countless moments that we would see each other again, he will still know the person behind such elaborate appearance that I partake, trying so hard to be someone that many would love and admire, still pretending to be someone I'm not. Nevertheless, after all these false pretenses, I realize that only through his unrelenting friendship and presence that I need not be someone I'm not, only to be who I truly am, and that is enough for him, and me. His friendship means so much to me; I could never see myself without him being there along the way.

17

VERSATILITY

When I first met Marcelo Sion, I told myself that I could never be friends with him, not that I don't like him or he may have something that appalls me, rather I have the first impression of him as being high maintenance. Although, he did not exhibit any indications that he's hiding or denying that what he is, different from the rest of the regular group that I so desperately wanted to be a part of, somehow, he had made it look cooler to be flamboyant, and I say this with terms of endearment. Moreover, at the same time, still maintaining a sense of dignity and respect from others, he wasn't afraid to express how he felt, which definitely shows on how he present himself in public as well as in private. Through his numerous articles, collections and autobiographical works that shows how he has grown tremendously from a shy whimsical person to a more confident, well-adjusted being. His mood changes from time to time, depending on a situation his in, one minute he'll pursue something that he'd never done before, shocking both Conrad and I, in the way he had acted. Surprisingly enough, it was something that we both also expected from him, for he is a man full of ideas and emotions that he needs to be in motion constantly. Like his all time idol, Madonna, he has somehow manage to change his looks and attitude to that of a chameleon, a creature capable of changing its appearance to blend with its surroundings, constantly being aware of its environment for predators, as well as, for nourishment, hoping to survive for another day, maybe even leave a legacy for others to ponder. Everyday of his life he has survived, thrived and even surpassed tasks that were difficult to accomplish if he wasn't the person he is, a person whose will is strong and whose loyalty is unmatched by any.

However, it's only now that I realized beneath all those flamboyant self expression lies a tortured soul, eager to be healed of its self doubt and the constant awareness of being watched and talked about by everyone around him; paranoia? I do not think so, everyone has experienced it in one form or another, of someone watching or staring at you. Somehow, every time that he's out in the open, where people seemed to mind their own way and not fully aware of what's going on in their every surroundings, Marcelo, without difficulty can somehow point out the person or group of people that seems to be staring and whispering words to each other about him. Things he might think and believe are against him, people whose stare give away significant and unpleasant meaning on how they perceive him as though they have never seen a creature not of this world. And their whispered words of defiance that seems to travel across my friend's path, hitting its intended target, without even thinking about the repercussions on the person they are talking about, followed by a menacing grin and laughter that made him more aware that they are indeed predators poking fun on its prey before they devour him body and soul. Heartbroken and disgruntled, Marcelo, would sometimes asked us if there was anything wrong with him, pointing out his face and asking again if there's something on him that would make those people stare and laugh at him. We'd say no, and tell him that their looks and appearances are of typical status and their manners are something to look down upon, that we were far better than any of them combined. For these creatures are people of profound insecurities in life, compared to us they are no match to our staggering physicality and mental superiority.

Nevertheless, the damage was done, no longer can he function in a way we know him to be, his spirit has been broken and no matter how much we tried to convince him that it's them who are at fault, it is never enough. They have somehow destroyed what he considered a sacred essence of himself: his individuality. To express himself the way he feels inside with no unwanted criticisms, especially from people who are not important to him. But then again, what he lacks in self-confidence, he more than makes up for his immense talents that only a handful of people are aware of, that is, to use his mind to deal and finish a situation that he never started. Vengeance is what his after, he implored the help of his friends to execute the plan that he meticulously thought of in such a way that he could let them know what it feels like tasting their own blood. Though words of wicked nature will be used by us to strike at the very heart of those who have defiled our sacred bond, what differs, is the manner it was carried out. For it was done with enough class and charisma they so immensely lack, where the prey becomes oblivious to its natural order and reach deep down within its primal nature, letting the predator in him take over and wreck havoc to those who have acted against his individuality. The predators are now the prey, unaware that a bolder, more cunning prey is lurking within their once dominated territory, ready to devour them and let them realize who and what their up against. Therefore, as his senses, heightened by the desire to inflict pain, located its rightful target, he began what is now would be defined as grace under immense emotions. He had executed them with such manner that they will never again hurt anybody, ever, for they have been stricken with shame and guilt for the things they have done to him. Moreover, the only way for Marcelo to show the things they did was to let them feel everything what it was like to be strike down in every fiber of their being, to experience the ugly part of a person's psyche, where hatred and envy dwells. In addition, to let them realize that there are consequences to every single actions they make, especially the ones where feelings are involved.

With the deed done, he smiled; he knows that it was for the best, and his glad that he was able to do it. Afterwards, he's back to his old self; happy, outgoing, with a touch of insecurity in his life, which we all know that we all possess, the Marcelo I knew and love. That's what I like about him, most especially the spider copulation that he's so into….but that's another story.

18

DENVER, CO

Anyone who sees and reads the title of this chapter from the book I'm writing, one might surmise that I am talking about a State in the US, about a simple town in the middle of nowhere, where people are a part of every community as much as the community is a part of every town. Doing the things that any ordinary person would be doing; chores, careers, activities, those kinds of things, but it's not about the town, or the people and the things they do that interests me. It's not even the place itself, Denver, Colorado, rather, it's about a bunch of people I knew when I was in high school that definitely caught my attention. They are quite rambunctious and mischievous, always getting themselves into a situation that predictably culminates in the principal's office. Being reprimanded and disciplined for their actions and behaviors, however, they were never suspended nor expelled from our school; they were just doing what any other teenage boys would do, whose hormones are way up the scale, off the scale in some occasions. Particularly, one guy in my class, Denver Anthony Manipon, a very hyperactive kid, in fact, much to his detriment, he gets into trouble a lot of times and yet he has the personality that I like about him. A very easy-going guy, where anybody can befriend him, although, I was quite shy at the time I started high school, I would later find out that I wouldn't be doing much work in getting to know him. Fortunately, for me, he was just sitting right beside me, since our seating arrangement goes by what our first letter of our last name starts with, we got to know each other right away. At first he had this tough attitude that he tries to show everybody, maybe he is, but sometimes I would notice that he'd only hang with a bunch of guys pretending to be in a gang and he would later move away from them if they were doing something that is not to his liking. Yet remaining close ties with them in case he needed a company he can count on. However, besides the toughness and macho attitude, he's a guy who's pretty much can function all on his own.

What I like about this guy is his innate sense of assurance of himself. He knows how to present himself both physically and sensually, oozing with such sex appeal that makes me wonder how the hell he does it. He's like 'fonzy' from happy days, only he doesn't act very tough but tough enough that he can hold his own, or does he sprout words of coolness where everyone would be mimicking to make themselves look and sound cool. In his own right, he is a cool guy, and as a matter of fact, I wanted to be like him, a tough guy that gets respect from everybody and emanates coolness that anybody would want to be like. Oh yeah, he's also good-looking, not that I'm falling over him, let me clear that up. As a guy, I can appreciate someone who's well endowed both physically and sexually, things that I definitely lack. However, I wasn't aware of his extreme coolness and the eagerness to be like him, back when I was more into my own personality. My friends and I hang with each other all the time, doing what we call cruising along the crowded malls, to find anything and anyone interesting. Excited and eager to add a little spice to our already boring day, occasionally, someone would eventually catch our attention and the hunt begins. We try our best to get theirs but to our dismay, our day ends up when one of us started walking away, and usually it's them that put the distance between us. Somehow, we never did realize that all we have to do was to look closer at home; our school has many good-looking people. People with qualities that set them apart from others, sometimes to the point that most of them hang with each other's, making them stand out even more. Denver definitely has those qualities that I notice about him, though, he may not be aware of his features, he is in fact one of the people I admire the most, not for his mental prowess or the ability to score with lots of women of his liking. Rather, the physicality that he exudes, he's a manly man, and girls go crazy for that, I would want to have what he has, the charisma and the confidence he has of himself, to do whatever he thinks is best for him no matter what the outcome it may be.

Back then, these things never caught my attention, I shied away from him, knowing that anything that are not in accordance with my principles, is something that I don't have to accept. He looked tough, he acted tough and sometimes he even talked tough, qualities that made me not want to be his friend. Yet somehow, I am drawn to him, wanting to have a friend like him, to get to know each other from each other's perspective. For the first three years of high school, we would just see each other, never really trying to be closely acquainted with the other. Rather than be friends, we just try to be classmates, minding our own business, trying to get along and finish a project. We never quarreled nor disliked each other, we just have qualities we didn't see in each other to go further than being classmates, he has his own friends and I had mine, however, by the end of our final year, we would share the one thing that made us both closer to each other than ever before.

He was in a different class by the time we hit our fourth year. Our final year was to be a year where we could just relax and let the days pass by without really working as hard as we did before. We were stable enough academically and slacking off wouldn't hurt any of us, our NCEE (SAT) were finished and we're in the process of preparing for our graduation ceremony. So working our butts off to get better grades wasn't really a priority since it'll be the last time that we'd be doing all these. That means we have a lot of free time in our hands, which made us do more crazy things that we normally wouldn't be doing, but it was also a time when our curiosity were abundant, to experience something new and bold, especially certain things that were quite forbidden for us to do. Acts of defiance against our natural state of being, we couldn't resist anyway since our raging hormones were taking over our own bodies, telling what we should be doing even if we know that it's against our beliefs. Add to the fact that we were on a stage wherein trying to figure out who we are and what or who we like was as important as trying to fit in a place where you are judge by your appearance. Peer pressure was definitely a big factor in determining what we should believe in, importantly, when everyone's telling you that sex is a natural thing. Moreover, when guys do it all the time, maybe so, but they didn't tell me those guys do it with other guys as well. That they weren't ashamed of anything, although they wouldn't voluntarily admit the fact that they were actually doing it, instead, they'll just deny or ignore the situation until it dissipates into nothingness. After all, its high school and news lasts only but a fleeting moment, however, if somehow, someone gets a word out and they confronted the person to gather detailed information of what it was like having someone do it besides you, they would only say that it's normal. Oral sex was in fact, according to many, not really sex, just a simple experimentation, and they believe that like kissing, it doesn't involve any form of penetration. It's a perfect excuse of not getting anyone hurt or worse pregnant, everybody's happy. No one would dare come forward and let it known that guys were thinking about it, they were all talks and no actions. Nevertheless, the fact is, everyone was curious about how it would feel like having a person mouth another person's thing. I hear them joke about it all the time, about the times they were involved in a simple sexual rendezvous with a girl, telling everyone who are willing to give their undivided attention, the detailed accounts on how it happened and the emotions involved. However, these are all tall tales signs that events never really happened, that they never really were involved in an uncensored situation, except one that is.

Rumor has it that there's this two guys during a Christmas party held at a schoolmate's house, somewhere along the serene compound of an upper middle class neighborhood, who got together and did what no one dared cross-over. That is, to pay respect to another guy's well endowed masculinity and let him swallow his pride, basking in his full frontal glory. It was a remarkable sight as rumors float around, complimenting its well-intended target, but also placing shame on a particular person involved in such a very sensitive situation. Neither the two involved told anyone and yet as their classmates realizes that during the said party that a couple of their guests were out of sight for quite sometime, they knew that something was happening behind a door that was kept tightly locked. Hoping that no one would enter and compromise a situation that was pre-planned the moment Denver Anthony Manipon walked in at the party and realized as he shook the hand of a guy whose been keeping his distance in check for sometime. Moreover, much to his surprise and happiness, he uttered the words with such eagerness and anticipation; "I didn't know that you're here, Melvs?"

From that moment, I knew what he meant, the look on his face to find out that I was there, even though I wasn't part of his class anymore, and that I only came along upon the request of a friend. It gave me a sense of awareness and absolute certainty that that night something will definitely happen between us. We both had eerie feeling that somehow we're trying to sense each other. Is he thinking what I'm thinking? We waited for an opportune moment to disclose our want, he held me on my shoulders, as he guided me towards a room that somewhat familiar to both of us. It wasn't the first time we were inside a bathroom; in fact, it was in the school bathroom that he first shared his friend with me. He was how should I say this, gifted. He wanted to see what I got, but reluctantly I declined, thinking I was particularly embarrassed to show it to somebody else other than myself. We closed the door behind us, but as it turned out, it was missing a part that we considered an integral part in our situation, a bolt, to shut it from the inside. Therefore, we made do with what we had and proceeded to go on with what we've planned. We almost did it, however, we both declined, thinking it's not the right place, so we both agreed that the bathroom was not sufficient enough for us. We came out and tried another room, much larger and spacious; there were no beds or furniture. Just some weights and exercise equipments, he found a place close to the window where he can lay down and rest, as we discuss the works that we needed to accomplish. Finally, we did what we came for, mission accomplished.

Suffice it to say, that the experience was quite a revelation for both of us, especially for me. Details will be kept hidden from prying minds, although my closest friends know what went on. It has somehow changed me in a way I never felt before; I can see things differently in a perspective of a person whose innocence was partly lost but never shattered. For even though, we were both just turning sixteen and on the verge of finding our own path through the experiences we've encounter, I have somehow gained something out of that experience. I experienced love and affection, and understanding, most of all a revelation.

19

G.F.R.S.

Gilbert Francis R. Susulin was the one person in high school I became extremely obsessed with, not just for the single attribute or feature he has, or the multiple talents he possess. Rather, it's about everything he is, he's a guy who's absolutely perfect in every way. A God-given looks and Adonis-like features that undeniably only he possess, an intellectual mind that has proven itself time and time again as he continued to maintain and surpass a grade that I can never attain. Most of all, a social skill that to many are of envy, he doesn't really have to do anything to get attention or get into a conversation, neither does he need to utter a single word to start a conversation. All he has to do is stand at a corner and people are drawn to him, people approach him as if they know him, making statements and giving gestures that sometimes made him give a smile that certainly melts the hearts of every girl he meets. To them it's like meeting someone famous. To know some-one of such physical caliber and a charisma worn with such precision, one might think if this guy truly exist, or did he discovered the secrets on how to use such God-given gifts to his advantage. To get what he wants just by a flick of a finger, or a nod, or even a simple smile that would turn anyone into his forsaken slave. I don't think anyone would mind being his slave; in fact, they would probably jump at the chance to be with him, to be his friend and maybe, even more.

Is he really that good looking, that charismatic? To have certain things fall into place just by who you are and how you look. I would definitely have to answer, yes! I have seen him and it was like looking at a person of perfection; physically, mentally and socially all rolled into one. If Denver is a person who gives out an aura of manliness, tough exterior but also having a keen sense of being sensible to others, Gilbert is a person whose not only all that but more. His fair skin is only match by his boyish looks and a smile that seems to never tire, and two birthmarks at the side of his right eyebrow that has people staring, not because of its simplicity or its size. Rather on its unique combination of colors that make them different from any other birthmarks: small, rounded, blue and green marks that have everyone in awe, creating a certain distinctiveness that allows himself to be the center of everyone's attention. It is as though, those were a sign from God to be the bearer of wonderful news that he is indeed one of a kind. Sculpted from clay and formed into a person, who not only possesses the physical attributes of every Greek mythological hero perfect in every way, but also acquiring the skills and charisma of a boy whose mere presence emanates innocence and playfulness and the innate ability to get along with almost everybody.

These are the feelings you get whenever his close by, the magnetism that draws everyone towards him is so intense, one can never resist, but to let themselves be captured by his embrace. Incessantly conveying a maddening sense of wanting to be near him, to be like him, only to realize that you are one of many whose existence revolve around many other obstacles, preventing you from reaching a heavenly body that has its resources cut off from you by the sole fact that you will never be like him. Sadly, this is true, as much as I wished and wanted to be like him, to have what he has, both physically and everything else that makes him what he is. I will always be reminded by the constant teasing that I get from the people who believe that I have a thing for him. That every look, every smile, and every question I ask about him and the things that of interest to him is a step that will eventually lead to us hanging out together, doing what in their foul minds are acts of defiance against our nature. However, it was never my intention or desire to have something that would result in anything but a good and warm friendship between two cool people, to get to know each other, even though I know for a fact that someone like me can never be friends with someone like him. Our worlds are far apart, destined to be separated forever, bound by an invisible force that tells me to keep my distance and let the gods be what they are born to do, that is, on a pedestal for everyone to see and admire, and aspire to be. Yet, it has prevented from doing so; for there are malicious minds wanting to destroy what I hope would be my chance to get to know him, even for a brief moment. Their inferior minds couldn't understand that the feelings I have are not of deceit and lust, where I could be in a position to take advantage of a person whose intentions are pure, but of respect and hope. Hope that he could also see in my heart that I only wanted to have a sense of what it's like to be him, to walk in his footsteps and feel the sensation of crowds reaching for your affection. The intensity of such power that I might wield would certainly be overwhelming for someone like me, who've never known to be in such a situation, but it's not going to be received with regrets, rather of anticipation and eagerness. For only when I become him, will I know what it is that makes him different from everyone else; maybe, I could do something about it. Moreover, to achieve something that could put me close to his caliber.

Such an enormous challenge, an impossible wish even for a guy who hopes and dreams that one day he'll wake up one morning and find him in someone else's shoes. I almost gave up, to have a chance to talk to him and let myself be heard and accepted. I got tired of all the constant mockery and untrue statements that people keep throwing at me, so I gave up. However, little did I know that another force is at hand, manipulating what fate has bestowed upon me, already putting events into motion that would guarantee myself in a position that will eventually lead to the one thing I've wanted the most in life. The moment I realize that, I am a child of faith, to trust in His name and let the rest fall into place. The burden that I was carrying lifted from my shoulders, replaced by whispered words of comfort and understanding. I am now at his grace, I was not disappointed.

A year of many struggles and taunts of trying to get a piece of knowledge from a person I admire the most, lead to a resounding despair. The final year of high school knowing he exists and within grasp was something I was willing to put my life on hold just to let him know that I, too, existed. Yet there was not enough time, our time in high school was nearing its end and I have not yet done anything to let myself known. That is, until He intervened, my prayers were answered. Though, we did not have the sufficient time to let each other be acquainted during high school, the times we've spent in college basic training was more than enough to accommodate whatever was lacking back then. We got to know each other very well, that we became good friends, meeting every Sunday, and if time permits, we got to chat about everything from the time we were in high school to the moment we realized that our lives will change the instant we took upon ourselves the chance of becoming who we are destined to become. That everything changes, even the people you know and the friends who've been there the longest. We learned that change is a part of life that we can never control, even if we wanted to. I wanted to stay there in that moment a little bit longer, to let time stand still. Nevertheless, as everything else that lives, there's an end. Our moment was ending, and it was enough for me. For I was able to walk in his footsteps and realize that I am not missing anything; we both were living a life that is not so different from any other person we know. We were just kids trying to figure out what we wanted from life, and I've learned that you won't always get what you want, that everything has a reason and everyone has a pur-pose, no matter how faint life gives you. But if for a moment you were given a chance to live a life that is different from the one you're leading, drown yourself into that experience and fill yourself with all the emotions that comes along with it, for it only last but a fleeting moment. I was fortunate to know what it's like to have someone you admire share his experiences and aspirations, as well as his struggles and frustrations with me. We may not see each other anymore, he had taken the path that he's destined to lead and I have taken my own, but I have relived that single moment over and over again, through the memories we shared together. And that my friend, will never change.

20

NO STONE LEFT UNTURNED

There comes a point in my life that I need to deal with what has been bothering me for as long as I can remember. The things that I've always keep asking myself and the feelings that keeps on hounding me, through my constant interactions with people I know and the people I just met. I've dealt with this subject a few times before, however, by the end of each chapter, I leave an opening that keeps people wondering whether I am truly being serious about it, or am I just trying to keep it together, holding back key information for as long as I can. Stalling and sometimes changing the subject until I'm ready to come up with a better way of letting everybody know what I am trying to let them piece together, a puzzle, that has been intricately woven to disguise a hidden agenda that I've been keeping to myself. Hoping that no one would suspect a lifestyle so confusing to someone like me and a subject matter that may bring a profound reaction from people when they realize that I am living a life that is far from what they expect it to be. Hiding behind a façade that to some is their only way of surviving from a world that is so critical and judgmental to persons that are different from what they perceive as anything but ordinary.

I am one of the few who stands on his belief that one day people will understand that being different has somehow made them unique from the rest of the crowd, and it's something to regard with pride, with head held up high. That if they were to change from who they are to what society dictates them to be, they'll only jeopardizing the very nature that makes them one of a kind. Moreover, to cower underneath a mask of concealment will only bring further misunderstanding and confusion to those people you're hiding it from and to yourself as well, believing that there is no better way but to conceal an identity that have been forcing itself out from within. Trying to let you acknowledge that it, too, exist within you and that without it, you are not complete. I have felt its tug ever so often, constantly trying to remind me that who I am is different from what I want people to see in me, that behind such intricate superficial layer of a typical boy next door type, lies a far more complicated machinery that has been trying to let its engine run. Only to be turned off every time that a comment or an awkward gesture is heard and seen once the word that I've been trying to bring up is spoken, for it is spoken with shame and disgust that prevents me from ever letting them know who I really am. Afraid that they would not treat me the same way once they find out, and they will never understand the reason behind the need to conceal. It was never my intention to hide but I am force to, in a way, since society dictates what is normal and what is not. Moreover, to be one that is different will only lead to isolation and despair; no one wants to be left out, alone in a place where everybody and everything are based on the fact that a society are built upon a foundation of ordinary people living in a world where a slight deviation from the norm is considered a freak. I am neither a freak nor ordinary. I am one of the majority of people living in a world where limitless ideas from people's different backgrounds and social upbringings are not only a norm but also an acceptable risk that one must take, for when one takes a risk, even knowing that it will not result in a fashion that they expect, it is still taken, for only through trials and mistakes that people learn and understand the reason behind its failure or success. Eventually they will learn to accept its impending result, no matter how it is perceive by one or by many. That no matter how I may have presented myself through their eyes, I am still the person who belongs to them, to a society that celebrates its unique assets and nourishes its members. They may resist at first, knowing that it is only a phase that one go through, hoping that by the end of such ordeal, I will go back to what I am. What I, and everyone else in my situation, was raised to be, and that is, a son to a mother and a father, a sibling to a brother or sister, a husband to a wife and a father to his children.

However, as the phase begins to dissipate far into adulthood, pass pubescence and the loss of innocence once feelings toward others, other than yourself and the family close to you are discovered and applied, you then realize that you are treading a path that is unfamiliar and uncharted. Yet somehow, you know that it is the right path to take, for it leads to your own fulfillment and freedom. Freedom from being hidden in the darkness of shame and guilt that it carries, freedom from all the emotions you keep inside, hoping it will stay inside once you mastered on how to control your own feelings. Freedom from not knowing if your love ones will still love you despite the way you are, and will still share the same interest as they have once they find out that I am what I am, and not what they know I am. That is, I'm a card carrying, a hundred percent, and no doubt about it, absolutely and totally gay. As cliché as that may sound, it's a term I used in order for people to understand that being gay is not what represents me, it is not what defines me as a whole. That beneath the exterior eccentricities and flamboyant behaviors is also a person who has a lot to offer, instead of being held back by people's narrow-mindedness and ignorance; I have talents and gifts that many ordinary people don't have and to express such talents in a medium that may be too different from theirs is something that makes me even more extraordinary. Moving away from the norm that most people tend to take, though, there's nothing wrong about that, it is something that I grew tired of, to look at the same object over and over again by the same people and still coming up with same points of view. Therefore, it is not what life is all about, rather to look at an object at different angles, at different dimensions and at different depths, definitely would arouse one's curiosity, further improving their analytical capabilities, hence, evolving to a more able minded person. Open to expanding its horizon through different settings and involving oneself to people of different backgrounds and upbringing, not afraid that I will be scorned and mocked for being different, rather welcomed with open arms not only for what I am but also for the things I can offer. Although, it takes but a second to integrate myself to people like me, since they too, have been to places and situations that I now am still discovering, providing me with adequate amount of knowledge on how to deal and cope with anything I encounter. Sometimes it takes a lifetime for others to be adjusted to what I am, denying that I am not what I say I am, and no matter how much I try to explain it to them, to show them every angle, give them every reason so they can understand and accept me, it is not enough. Therefore, it is a task that is so difficult to accomplish, for sometimes the result comes at a greater price, where the two parties involved end in a sour note, separated and not knowing how to get back on track. Back with their lives before the fatal announcement, rejected by them and disgusted by the fact that I'm not one of them. There are those who want to see me fail, to see my face down in the mud soaking in misery and despair, to feel ashamed that I have brought this all to myself. And maybe, I would change my mind and go back to what they know and believe that I'm suppose to, to live a life that they expect for someone like me to lead. A happy normal life with a family that I love and cherish, and children who will carry my legacy through the teachings I taught them and through the lessons that they will learn themselves as they tread through life's unexpected changes.

I can still do all that, be what they want me to be, and maybe even more. I can still have a family I love and cherish, only without a wife but a partner for life that shares my interests, my goals and aspirations. We can still have kids of our own where we can be role models for them, play with them and let them have their own goals in life without really pushing them to something they don't want. Giving advises and opinions when needed, and most of all, be there for them when at times where troubles and heartaches seems abundant, a shoulder to lean on and show them that people are different from one another and accept them for who they are. As I said, I'm no different from any other person who aspires to be somebody, and to share that with someone. I am what I am and I can never change that. Moreover, who I am is a person you see everyday, you mingle with me as day and night passes, with no knowledge that you have met and befriended a guy who looks no different from everyone else, only that I am a guy who is attracted to the same gender. People and society may still cringe whenever they hear this statement, they may not accept me for what I am, but it too, shall pass. Someday soon, they will learn to accept and maybe even love the idea of me and everyone else like me, being different from them. They might want to get to know me and if they do, they might be surprise that I'm not that different. In fact, they might find out that what I am is in them, and what they are is in me.

I am what I am, and I am gay!

21

INNOCENCE LOST

As I got out of the room from a motel that I stayed in for a couple of hours, with a person I just met, I tried to feel my behind; gently and slowly, ouch! It's still sore from being fucked by a boy ten years younger that I am; he was just a teen-ager and I, a young man when I first laid my eyes on him, in a dark corner of a movie theater not far from where I used to live. It was a time when I was on a vacation trip back home and made it a point to myself that this time, I will have to get what I really wanted the most in my adult life, that is, to get laid by a boy or a man who resembles like a boy. It's just so happened that it was a seventeen year old who fucked me, and it was great! For me and for him as well, since I got to fuck him too! I've always been curious as to how it would feel like when your at the bottom of a sexual rendezvous, to find out where everything goes, where to hold onto, which one is up and what is down. Should it stay up, or does he hold it while being penetrated. I learned so much from that encounter, and its something I would definitely do it again if the occasion calls for it. A chance I will take by the horn, er, ass if need be.

It happened one fateful day, when I decided to go to my favorite place where everything and almost everybody can be something you desire. A place where people roam around, busying themselves with errands that they need to accomplish, where vendors sell newspapers, candies and other goodies, yet behind the counter lies far more interesting reading materials that will certainly arouse one's curiosity. Moreover, a place where students go and learn things that they may never get to apply once they venture outside their protected walls, and most of all, where teenagers alike dressed up like ordinary students, yet they have something more devious on goings behind such an intricate deception. Hiding behind an appearance that they have so meticulously created as not to arouse any suspicion from an unsuspecting people, whose sole intent is to bring them to justice, rather to attract possible clients that will definitely be stimulated by their innocently looking appearance and hell-bent on doing everything as to please their benefactors. The benefactors are then, so mesmerized by the encounter, willingly and generously hand them everything they have as though hypnotized by their innocently looking mate, completely under their control and not in control of their own faculties, it is somehow becomes a routine for this once shy boys. Yet through constant practice and learning the tricks of the trade out in the streets and through other, more experienced boys who have done this many times before, they have somewhat pinpointed the ones with enough dough, although undecided and confused, still possesses a staggering desire to get laid no matter who they get. It is so easy for them to manipulate and take advantage of these unsuspecting lustful clients. To collect the fee they so firmly established and handled in such a way that they are able to live through for a few more days with what they have collected. I bet that if they would ask to double their price, they probably would get it without so much of a difficulty, since their clients will surely hand over any price to anybody just to have a one-night stand with somebody that doesn't involve any commitments or responsibilities. What more can they ask for, if it is a student with qualities they desire the most, a boy whose developing body is an instant attraction all by itself, and whose untainted innocence in this flesh starved world of human craving is in itself a bait to those whose lust can never be satisfied or tamed by any means. Drawing attentions either from gay men, who may not look so desirable that their only means to satisfy the hunger is to hire someone willing enough to mate with them, even if it means paying their way into a comfortable yet expensive room. Also to dirty old guys whose lust can only be fulfilled by someone much younger, way younger than they are, to act as though a father figure to these boys, and yet it's their flesh that they crave for. Its like handing their children gifts so they will do whatever they want them to do, thinking they are in control just because they have the resources to give them anything they want, but in reality, it's the other way around. These boys are well aware of what they are doing from the very start, conniving and scheming their way into someone else's pockets, taking and possessing what they think is what they deserve. After all, it is their bodies that they're promoting, the ultimate weapon against any other offer or prize that one can possess. Who can resist such an offer? Such body devoid of all inhibitions and awkwardness, also emanating a sense of magnetism that draws anyone willing to be preyed upon by them, just look at their faces, their features, and imagine that they're in front of you naked, seeing them everything all in their glorious presence, the body that is within your reach. Moreover, wanting to do the things you have imagined and wished for, how can anyone resist? The temptation that is within your grasp, to know that once you have stepped inside a world unlike any other, a world you've never been, things will never be same again, ever.

Heck, I surely couldn't, resist that is. I was fortunate enough not to belong on either side of the category that I've mentioned before: the ugly gay guys and those who are old, dirty minded men. Not me, though, I was in my late twenty's when it happened, but I was lucky to look like a guy in his late teens. To pass easily as someone, who in the eyes of everyone, as a boy who still has plenty of growing up to do. It also gives me tremendous advantage not to arouse any suspicions of being a cradle snatcher, since I know that I like boys, in fact, I love boys! I prefer men also, although, I'm somewhat fussy when it comes to them, they need to possess certain qualities that I find in young boys; cuteness, charisma, physical features that makes them look like a young boy. I prefer them to be hairless, not too rough on the outside, and definitely a smooth well-defined body, like a boy. Does this make me a pedo? I don't know, I ask my very close friends on what they think of me with this obsession of mine, they kind of nodded their heads in agreement, made some remarks that tells me that I'm indeed a cradle snatcher. Although, often times they would agree with me on how I prefer boys since there are certain moments that they find it mesmerizing to see qualities that I see in them. Then they become obsessed, only for a moment, afterwards they go back to their own preferences, leaving me with my ultimate desire, boys.

Anyway, as I decided to pursue my goal of getting something out of this experience, I went to the said place and inside a movie theater, not to view the latest commercial feature that is heavily advertised, but be in a constant prowl, finding and looking for a potential candidate that could fulfill my desire. Hoping that the one I pick and choose will be someone I prefer, and would be willing to perform such task that will eventually lead to my satisfaction, stripped off all the inhibitions and limitations, going all the way to give himself to me willing and able, allowing myself to be a part of him. As I walked pass the hallway, leading to the main view room, I saw someone leaving as though not satisfied with what he thought was a good movie, although I couldn't quite make out his expression, I looked and stared at him for as long as I can, he walked passed me. Hoping he would give me something in return, he looked straight at me and continued walking, I got disappointed and embarrassed on what I just did. He might have thought that I was crazy, maybe scared him somehow, that's why he walked away. Thinking to myself, "Was that it? That it was over as fast as it began?" I tried to look back at where he went for the last time, hoping he'll come back-he did! At last, someone responded to my signal, which I've been told is a definitive way of letting them know that you're interested in them. He started walking towards me and still keeping his eyes on mine, my heart started racing as I began walking alongside of him to a semi-lit corner where we can talk. A strategy of some sort, maybe to somewhat familiarize ourselves with each other as well as to make out the face, whether the person standing side to side of each other is good-looking enough and able enough to pursue something that both of us are thinking about. Most of all, willing enough to satisfy our inner most craving, our hunger, the desire to have sex. Sex is what we both wanted, I felt attracted to him, and maybe he too, felt attracted to me, so we started making conversation on what we would like to do to each other. Setting limits and boundaries that at first we were awkward to discuss, hesitating and sometimes resisting some suggestions from both sides, especially from him. Maybe, it's his way of telling me that his fresh and untainted, that I need to be gentle and easy when it comes to such matter. I was just trying to find out if he's into things that I'm interested in doing, though not quite experienced in matters of four plays, I suggested it anyway, thinking he's willing and might somehow cave in to my suggestions. Not to discourage and frighten him, I buckled down and offered that we can do things that are simple and common, not so kinky and bizarre. He nodded, and smiled back at me, a smile that brought a profound meaning that I would later find out, once we had each other alone with no one to bother us as we exited the place as discreetly as possible. Knowing all eyes might be staring at us once they learned of how we will spend our brief, yet exciting and unrestrained moment.

Walking alongside the crowded streets of C.M. Recto, we blended perfectly as though friends that have not seen each other for a long time, while still maintaining a respectable distance from unsuspecting eyes. I asked if he knew a place we could stay in, not surprisingly, he knew somewhere close by and inexpensive enough that we can still be comfortable. I followed him from behind about two to three steps ahead of me, and pointed the alley that we will be entering. We went together and as I stepped toward the counter to hand over the appropriate amount for our suite, the bellboy gestured to follow him to our destination, as my potential and chosen mate followed from behind as though not knowing who I am. Still playing the innocent bystander, I guess. Upon reaching the door that will lead to the fulfillment of my desire, I paused for a moment to re-think of what I am doing. Should I go through with it? My morality starts kicking in and overcome my lustful desires, overshadowing all the planned encounters that I would be performing if I go ahead with it, to turn back from everything that I believed in, everything that I learned about the things a good Christian should be doing. That a child of faith need not involve oneself in ways that will certainly be a crucial factor in determining one's existence once the day of reckoning is at hand. Moreover, to know that once the key is placed on the doorknob that will open the gates of utter insanity, there is no turning back-somebody else decided how my fate should take place. The door opened itself as I stepped inside a room that is very much appropriate for somebody like us, there were no sentimental things that we could be attached to, only a plain and somewhat cold room that is furnished by a few things, you'd need in order to accomplish a task for a few hours you'll be spending. A phone, perfectly situated beside the bed if ever you need something else you might use during the course of your acquaintance, a television placed on a wall that shows erotic scenes to add to your already titanic emotions. However, if you decided to change your mind and feel that it's inappropriate for someone like you to do, the scenes their playing will definitely put you in the mood as fast as you can realize. In addition, it will make you forget everything once you laid your eyes on him; most importantly, a bed where everything you'll be doing is spent on, to give warmth to a cold sheet from the bodies that emanates so much intensity and desire, rubbing and caressing each other for comfort and excitement. We settled in nicely at our place and proceeded to the most comfortable area in the room, realizing that we needed to break the ice, I suggested to take a shower, and asked if I can set up a video camera to take clips of ourselves doing what we know would be a tremendous opportunity to get everything on tape. Especially for me, as a sort of souvenir for me take back home, he said yes without hesitation, and after he got himself a shower, laid on the bed that's already been occupied by a very nervous yet eager beneficiary. We were side by side on a queen size bed, as I started making conversation, suggesting what we should be doing. Out of nowhere, I bluntly asked whether he allows himself to be penetrated, if he likes to be fucked as well. I got aggressive and clearly wasn't thinking right; my emotions were very much in control. Everything I do or say are a product of my lust, something that I've never experienced before. I read every magazines, seen countless videos that would often culminate with me being alone in a room, with my hand on my cock spilling some moderate amount of creamy, sticky white juice that sometimes gets on my shirt with no one else around to witness and share my longing. I can satisfy myself every time I want or need to; all I have to do is watch the videos of guys doing one another, viola! However, the one thing I can never have is someone to share it with, knowing that when I finally come, someone's there to witness and feel everything I'm experiencing, until now that is. So the moment has arrived, I need to grab it by the horn, which is the sole reason that lead me to asking him if he likes someone inside of him. Expecting to hear a resounding no, instead, he turned his head towards me, smiled back, and said yes! No hesitation, no limitation, no boundaries, all gloves are off! I wanted to yell out of sheer joy that finally someone is willing to go all the way with me. I've been preparing myself for this moment, I've been ready my whole life, ever since I found out that I'm into them.

Without a word, I leaned towards him onto his awaiting nipples, ready to licked and sucked by my hungry lips and playful tongue with eager anticipation. I heard a soft moan coming from him as a response to my move; he liked it, so gave him more, circling his nipples with my tongue as I did my best to satisfy him and myself as well. Tasting him through his nipples was something I've never experienced before; I can't find words to describe such sensation. I sank deeper into him, and every time his moaning gets stronger and louder, his nipples were hard as a rock as my tongue slid in and out of my mouth trying to reach every corner, every crease of his still developing body. I found myself petting his neck, while his arms were around me, embracing me; I looked into his eyes and started kissing him. It's not a smack on the lips, or a tender kiss you give to a love one, rather a wet and erotic kind of thing, our tongues were fighting each other to see who get dibs on the other's mouth, where lips gets pushed and pulled as we try to out do the other in a kissing contest. I didn't even realized that he was already on top of me, kissing and licking my neck, going down to my nipples, as I looked at him open his mouth and pushed out his tongue out to receive my eager nipples, ahhh!, was the only sound heard all over the room. His good at what he do, making me realize that he may have done this before, although, at first he wasn't showing any signs that he's very much experienced. But it doesn't matter now; all that matter was the fact that I'm having a great time. I placed my hand over his head to give a full attention to my nipples, as it becomes harder and wider while he tries his best in giving it all. Then he leaned over my head and started kissing me again, this time his entire whole body was on top of me, my arms started to slide down his back onto his butt, squeezing them gently, trying to measure up his soft muscular behind. I have one thing in mind as of that moment, and that was to slide my finger in his ass; slowly and gently I pulled apart his butt to give some needed space for me to find and insert my finger into his hole. He knows exactly what I was going to do, he never gave a hint that he 's against such a thing, so I proceeded to caress his hole as not to overwhelm him so much with a pain so intense he may not want to continue. I slid my middle finger in and as he got used to its size, I pushed a little bit further and in return, gave a soft moan of

ecstasy. Already an inch inside, I could feel the warmth that his hole was produc-
ing, wanting some more response, I pushed and pushed my finger into his hole
further and further in until I reached the end of my finger, I was completely
inside of him, while he continued on licking my nipples and kissing my neck. His
body was making a gesture as though he was both in pain and in utter sexual
completion, I kept my finger in and still to give him some needed rest from a
moment's ecstasy and to make him comfortable and let his hole adjust. Maneu-
vering with such ease, I pulled my finger little by little enough to stir a reaction
from him, but not too much as to completely taken it out, once I felt that my finger was nearing its end, I stop and continued pushing it once more. This time I
heard a moan unlike any other, as though his telling me that he wants more,
holding onto my body for support while trying to adjust to such tremendous feeling and at the same time trying to satisfy my need. Not to be out done by his
experienced moves, I pounded his ass again with my finger that's starting to get
lonely.

I was still aware that the camera was continuously taking clips of us making
our every move, with that in mind; I made sure that every fantasy I can remember
and wanted to execute were caught on camera. Whenever I feel like wanting to
reminisce about our brief encounter, not only do I remember the unbridled pas-
sions we shared, but also I can visually appreciate the event up close through the
technological breakthrough that will surely be a defining moment in my life. A
coming of age, of some sort, wherein I have successfully surpass a threshold of
sexual innocence or ignorance, from a world beyond that of just being a person
looking in front of a television alone, trying to satisfy myself to a sexually charged
being that have had the opportunity in bringing one's desire to reality. He may
have done this before, but from the moment he said yes to an uncensored and
unrestrained passion that would result in both of us having the focus of an
unmanned camera, we realized who was really in charge. We were just pawns to
our innermost longings, yet I was trying to make sure that every view of his body
and myself, and every position were viewed on camera, he may not even be aware
that a camera was rolling; he just did what he does best. It was clear that he was
drowning in complete state of utter insanity. And he's taking me with him,
plunging deep into our deepest darkest craving. I am not going to resist, I
accepted him with open arms and legs up high.

I had so many things going in my mind, and the one thing that keeps on pop-
ping in, telling me that it's time for me to realize finally the one desire I've been

aching to find out, to be on the receiving end. I was reluctant at first to let him know that I'm ready to receive him with full cooperation. Having no experience in a manner that would put myself into something I may regret in the long run, and it may very well cause severe pain once the deed is done. I just kept quiet for the meantime and busy myself by continually plunging his ass with now two fingers, he didn't budge or moved away as I increase the number of fingers I place inside him, as his hole also increased in size to accommodate an increasing human dildo. Only a soft groan heard as my speed intensified in pushing and pulling my fingers inside an ass that's starting to take its toll on me. I can't take it anymore! I want him to give it all to me, to have him inside me. Throwing away all my worries and inhibitions and putting my trust into a person that will soon give me the ultimate desire I've longed to acquire. Finally, I asked him whether his ready to give it to me, to fuck me. He took my cock out of his mouth and looked down towards me, as I looked at him with anticipation, he answered, "absolutely."

This is it! There's no turning back now, I have surrendered myself to him. As he gets ready to perform a task that he has done many times before. With a somewhat reluctant expression, I handed him a condom to use for protection, as I repositioned myself on top of the bed while also telling him with absolute certainty that this is my first to be penetrated, and he needs to take it as gently as possible. He nodded and continued putting on the piece that will certainly help both of us in realizing our goal without any worries that we don't want to pass along, I surely wouldn't want it, and so I came prepared. Wasting not one bit, he was ready to penetrate me as I held my legs up high over his head and rested them on his shoulders, telling him once more to take it easy and think about the repercussions it might have on me if ever he was to do it forcefully. So it begins, raising my butt up in the air just a few inches off the bed to receive his cock, he slowly guided it with his right hand into my awaiting hole. I felt the head touched my ass and continued pushing it in, arrggghh!!!, was my response as I screamed in absolute pain and instinctively holding back his legs from thrusting it forward with arms stretched to its limit, preventing his cock from going in. I told him that it hurt so much and he needs to let me rest for a little bit, his cock wasn't totally inside, just the head, yet it was more than enough for me to illicit such a response. I was very anxious and in pain while he tries to hold back his lust in order for me to adjust to such a big cock. Not wanting to let go of his leg, I told him to take it out for now and let his fingers penetrate my hole, he agreed and took his cock out while I moaned and started to introduce his playful fingers inside me. I felt a little ecstasy as he performed the task that a few times has done it to myself. Eager to have him inside me again, I told him he could once again fuck me and not let my emotion distract him from doing what he was set out to do, to which he obliges without hesitation. Holding his legs as he continued to push his huge cock inside my already sore ass, I told him to stop and again held on to his thighs with such tremendous effort not to let him in me. I was ready to give up and let it just move on, I don't think I can take it anymore. The pain was so severe for someone like me to bear, I told him to take it out and do something else besides doing what gives me so much pain. Moving my head from side to side to somewhat alleviate the pain that seems endless, and wanting him to take his cock out, I felt a pair of hands gently grab my hands that was holding his legs aback and managed to interlock our fingers together as though wanting to hold me in someway. He lifted my arms up in the air, forcing me to let go of his legs, which might have been bruised up, from the tight hold I had placed on it, he then slowly pushed his entire cock inside me. I continually screamed and moaned the entire time he was doing it, gripping his hands so tightly with every move his cock makes, inch by inch, it entered my hole like a sharp knife piercing my body. Yet every time my hole gets stretch to accommodate the size of his cock, I've become more and more accustomed to its immense structure, making it more pleasurable for me as the pain becomes less intense. I tried to feel how far along his cock was by squeezing my ass with every rest he made to give me a moment's peace. I thought my pain would be over once he had his whole cock in, with a last pushed that puts his cock inside me, I gave a final groan that sends me into oblivion. He's finally inside and I can feel his entire cock occupying a portion of my ass, he took his hands away from mine and leaned on top of me. Our bodies somewhat fused together as he proceeded to move back and forth, rubbing his entire body against mine and at the same time I can feel his cock coming in and out of me. Every moan I made was a response from every plunge he makes, he asked me if was okay, thinking that I didn't want to go through with this after experiencing so much pain, I said I was all right and was pleased that he's concerned about my well-being. I was thrilled that he didn't listen to me and abandoned his desire to give what I wanted in the first place.

I wasn't aware that my legs weren't on his shoulders anymore; instead, it was up in the air with no one supporting them. Then it caught me, so this is how it looks and feels like when someone fucks you, unconsciously signaling myself to assume the position that many have tried and succeeded. It wasn't so difficult to execute such feat even for a novice like me; rather it's how long you can endure such manner where you are constantly pounded by the sheer force of momentum of his musculature that you receive every successful entry of his awesome, undeniably huge dick. You get exhausted after a while, your legs get numb a little from being up in the air for quite some time, and you need to give them some rest, but once you put them down on the bed, you'll have to bring them up again since that position makes it comfortable for you. Instead of swinging it up, I gently wrap my legs around his waist and legs, also to familiarize myself intimately with his entire sweat drenched body. An expert equestrian was riding me, while my hands were sliding back and forth on his back, touching and caressing his butt, hoping to reach his hole in order for me to do same thing to him. I settled for what I have and enjoyed his ass fucking and nipple licking, then he uttered the words that I've been waiting to hear. "I'm coming," were the words that came out of his mouth, as his cock spurted out the culmination of his sexual plateau inside me under a well-protected latex sheath, which was the only thing that separates us from completely being a part of each other. With each contraction of his cock makes, I tried to sense something that would give me an indication that's his actually cumming, other than the long, deep breathing he gave, I couldn't make out from any of it, maybe because he was still pounding my ass back and forth with every squirt his cock makes. He was finished cumming, yet he was still fucking me and I was still holding onto him. His movements got slower and slower, a sign that his done. He took a few more second before taking out his huge cock and I felt it come out of my ass, I gave a soft moan and looked at him, he smiled. I felt a sigh of relief and satisfaction for having his cock out and at the same time, for having the ultimate fantasy fulfilled. My concern now was my ass was so sore that it felt like there is still a cock inside it, the hole was well opened up to the size of his cock that I was afraid it might stay like that forever. I touched my ass and it hurt, and I ignored the pain for a while. As he came out of the bathroom fresh from after a shower, he lay down beside me and I reached for his nipples and caressed both of them, placing him into a deep frenzy. I asked him whether he was ready to be fucked, he said just to wait a while for he needed a moment to recuperate. I waited, thinking that he might change his mind and not succumb to our agreement, and knowing from experience that after a person comes, his libido drops dramatically, making him less likely to perform and finish his intended service. Therefore, I tried to expedite his mood by licking and sucking his nipples, making him more lustful and sensual to the situation, and more agreeable. I asked him once more if the situation warrants him getting penetrated from someone like me, who was careful not exhibit a look of desperation, but with enough firmness that he may succumb to our agreement. He said yes, and told me to put on the other condom. While he's licking and sucking my nipples to put me in the mood, I began putting on the protection to my already hard rock cock, then I told him he should sit on my cock. With his left hand, he grab hold of my cock enveloped in a slippery condom, and lifted up his left leg, swung it over my body to position him right onto my awaiting cock. He opened up his hole as he guided my cock into his ass, and forcing it inside. I stared at him, looking for a reaction he might give; he cringed as it went in, only for a moment, and started to move his body that gave me an extreme sense of satisfaction that finally, I'm at the other end of a two-way sexual encounter. To experience what it's like to be on top of somebody else, giving them what they previously had given me. I reached out for his nipples with mouth, further intensifying our already burgeoning desire, and all of sudden my cock came out. I was flabbergasted! Worried that he might get tired of doing it over again, I told him he can lay down and I'll be doing it the old-fashioned way. Not wanting him to walk away from an opportunity to be penetrated by a neophyte, who emanates so much desire and enough knowledge from watching all those videos, it made me want him more. I decided to give him some piece of my lips and tongue; I slid my tongue up his body and onto his hard nipple, and down to his navel where he gave a moan while he raised his mid-section indicating he liked what I did to him. This made my cock rock solid once more and ready to finish what I've started, I grabbed his right knee pit and flexed it up towards him, giving me ample space to slide my cock inside his ass. He then took his left leg and held it place onto his stomach, ready to accept me, the mere sight of him positioned in that manner. Where his legs and feet are up in the air, where his arms and hands are holding them in place, his body lay flat on bed, nipples sticking up his chest and his head looking at me, waiting to receive something from me, not knowing that his also giving me the one thing that I may never experience ever again. It is a sight that brings joy to my life, where I'll always remember forever, if not for the experience but for the brief moment, we've shared together. So I gave it my best, grabbing hold of my dick and guiding it towards his hole, looking at him ever so often to see his reaction while I slide my cock inside him. It's almost in, one more push and I'll be completely inside him. I gave a hard push on my cock around his tight hole, then he cringe as it hurt and at the same time loving every minute of it. At last, I'm in! My cock was definitely touching his ass for I felt my hair and my skin touch his widely opened butt, I paused for a moment, then started to move my hips back and forth, constantly watching him from a point I've never been in. His head moved from side to side as I let my cock in and out of his hole, my hands was still holding his knee pit spreading them as wide as I can. I could never imagine that his body could able to sustain such a position like that for a long time, I can feel my cock inside him completely, and his hole was warm and somewhat slippery, and very tight. He didn't give any indication that he was in pain like the one I did, even though I was ramming his ass as deeply as I can. He has definitely done this before, his hole has gotten used to the different sizes of cocks that continues to get inside him that he never get hurt when someone fuck him. And I'm definitely one of them, to him; I'm probably just another statistics to his ever-growing clients. However, it doesn't matter. I'm fucking him for goodness sake, a boy. I am fucking a boy! What more can I ask, but to enjoy the moment and bask in the glory that for once and maybe forever I got what I came for.

I was afraid that while fucking him, my cock would lose interest and go limp on me, and I may end up with a frustrated mate, thinking that I have no idea what the hell I'm doing. It did pop up in my mind about such thought, then again, I looked at him reacting to my every thrust, and all the worries went away. In fact, the experience that I was ready to shoot my load inside him mesmerized me intensely. "I'm coming," were the words that came out of my mouth, almost reaching the pinnacle of our sexual rendezvous. 'I'm almost there," were the words that followed, setting up the situation and getting him ready for the culmination of my desire, faster and faster I went, ramming him and thrusting my hips as I reached my plateau. 'Haaahh," was the word I uttered as I kept my cock very still, deeply inside him. I didn't move my hips just the way he did when he was coming, I wanted to make sure he felt the sensation of my cock pumping my load inside his tight, warm ass. He gave me a moan and a brief sigh of pain when he felt my cock contracted, widening his hole while I shoot my warm semen inside the condom that protected us from any unwanted diseases. I kept still until I finished coming, I stared at his face and looked at his body drenched with perspiration coming from him and me as well. Slowly, I moved my hips back and forth, again letting him know that I wasn't finish with him. Repeatedly, I continued on fucking him until my cock slowly went soft and with one move, I took it out of his hole, looking at his ass and face while I was taking it out. From that view, I saw his ass wet from the sweat and from the natural lubricant that the body produces, most importantly, his ass was somewhat sore from being stretched and rammed continuously. However, instead of lying down on bed to recuperate from such an ordeal, he turned around, got up, and proceeded to the bathroom to freshen up, as though nothing seems to hurt him. He took it a stride, as natural as breathing. I removed the condom and went with him inside the bathroom, threw it in the can, looking at him while water ripple down his beautiful young body. I realized that he was completely taken in with our encounter for he was stroking his cock and ran his hand over his body.

We both came out and started getting dressed, I turned off the camera and proceeded to pack my things, when he suddenly tapped my shoulder and handed me a piece of paper containing telephone numbers of people I might want to try to call. Telling me that if I ever wanted to have another rendezvous with another guy, all I have to do is call one of his friends from the list he gave me. He smiled at me and I said, "absolutely!' As I looked around the room, I gave a smile and walked away, bringing with me the experience that I will forever remember and cherish. To know that one time in my life, I overcame self-pity and regret, and got what I wanted. Moreover, believing that I have what it takes to pursue something once I set my mind into what I believe that I am ready to partake. That boy gave it to me, his body, his innocence, his name. I will always remember Eric; it was him that gave me my best experience ever.

22

A CHANCE ENCOUNTER

By the time I came to this place, I realized that I would be leaving behind people that somehow had made my love life quite meaningful. I won't be able to see them take off a piece of their garment which would definitely make my heart pound an extra beat, pupils dilated and senses on high gear once a good looking guy passes by. Only through the memories and pieces of cut out pictures I shared with them in moment of loneliness and lust will stand as a reminder that I'm going to a place far away, where I won't be able to get a hold of them. Sadness fills my heart as I said goodbye to my 'friends' to venture to another world I'm quite reluctant to go. But then again, I later find out that this world has much more to offer than I realized, for they have many individuals whose looks are far, far better than the ones I'm used to, they have qualities and features that I can only dream of. A higher form species and somehow I became completely drawn to them, although even before I came to this place, I was quite enamored in people of their kind, through the movies and shows they were in that I came to watch and love. However, it was obvious that none of them resides anywhere near my town, so I settled for what I have until I set foot on this world. People of their race, Caucasian, are so beautiful and good looking, one might think that it's a place where dreams live and fantasy dwell, yet I was neither dreaming nor fantasizing, little did I know that I was in for a big surprise.

Anthony Deleva came up to me and introduced himself, while I shook his hand in astonishment, I was nineteen at that time. He never knew this, but he became my 'friend' in times when I can no longer hold my desire and end up thinking about him, releasing the built up feelings I have for him. He was thirteen, unaware that I was falling in lust over him, still in spite of our age difference we still became close friends. Anthony was definitely good-looking Italian guy with blue eyes and dark brown hair, and a body that gives me a sense of excitement whenever I see him half-naked with his upper body exposed to me, drooling like a hungry wolf. And often times I see him drenched in perspiration that would make me want to come over and wipe everything off with my bare hands, I was so mesmerized by his boyish charisma that all I can think of back then, was him. I even went out of my way just to be with him by taking him to the shore, romping around in his beach shorts. There are also moments when he'd ask me to cut his hair, to which of course I jumped at the chance for I will be able to see his body covered only by my eagerness to let him take off his shirt, while I stared at his beautiful smooth chest as I clipped his hair. Jokingly, I would pinched his nipples to satisfy my need to experience the feelings involved when touching a boy's body and watching the reaction he gives. The resulting consequence of my action was the fact that he'd do the same with me, we started horsing around with each other like boys whose not only left home alone, but also most importantly, boys whose hormones are out of control, mine especially. I went as far as pulling his boxers down a little to see his nice smooth baby crack, man! Just the sight of him in front of me doing what any normal teenage boys would do; playing, teasing, flirting with anybody that's willing to take his behavior, it gives me a sense of wanting to be like him and the same time wanting to forever be with him.

The feelings I have for Anthony is quite new to me, yet somehow it feels and looks familiar. As I look back to the days I've been in the same situation and at the moment where I am drawn completely to a person that I considered someone I admire and love, I can only think of one person, his name was Gilbert. I did the same things, felt the same way, and thought the same ideas with Anthony as I did with Gilbert. Only with Gilbert, we were both the same age, sixteen to be exact, when I started feeling and wanting the things he has and possess, and at the same time yearned to be always be by his side. It was as though cupid struck his arrow to my heart, bestowing me the person I longed for, but also opening the forbidden Pandora's Box containing the dreaded emotions particularly envy and lust towards him. I guess it was okay back then, since I was young and not particularly interested with the consequences that comes along with it, but now it's different. I was turning twenty and Anthony, on the verge of puberty, when I first laid my eyes on him and felt so much desire for someone like him. Although, he was just a boy, it did not stop me from wanting him and also to be like him. It's confusing I know, yet I understood how I felt, which also made me realize that someone like him can never be attained, even if I wanted to. I couldn't, for there are severe consequences to whatever action I might take, the distance in our age alone is in itself an obstacle that could lead to profound punishment I dare not cross. Therefore, I just look and stare, and wish for someone like him to be a part of me. An acceptable compromise but not completely satisfying no matter the situation I'm in, he's so within my reach yet so far that I would not dare lay my hands on him. Where does that leave me? Nowhere I guess, except, to know who I really am hiding it.

I can't say or write anything else about Anthony, only the ones that I've already described through the feelings I had and the desires of my heart. Somehow, the only way for others to understand what I'm going through, is to see and experience what it's like to be me, to have the emotions bared in front of you whenever a product of your lust and want passes by. You have no idea whether to act on it, or force yourself to be restrained from such an enormous challenge of concealing what you really feel inside, whether you are into guys or just plain confused. That you could somehow be something more than you actually admitted a few minutes ago, not just, what you have revealed to the world, rather, there's a deeper, darker side into your psyche. That somehow, somewhere you have already taken the steps that would lead to your dreaded conclusion, yet you still keep on telling yourself and everybody for that matter, that you are what you say you are, and ignoring what you really feel whenever boys are around. Somehow, I've already created a pattern to my desire starting from the years in high school up until now, where my preferences in the same sex are concerned.

You know what I'm talking about, about the likes and dislikes I have when it comes to guys, er boys. Thing is, what should I do? Do I tell, or keep in hidden inside, never to divulge it to anybody, ever. I'm afraid if I do tell, it will be my downfall.

23

COTERIE

Anthony may be the first one that caught my attention, specifically the desire to have him all for myself. In a world full of untainted potential, culminating to an event where I was able to partake in occasions of merriment with others like him, I got fortunate to acquire some souvenirs through stolen pictures I've taken during our three-day rendezvous to the shores of Pt. Pleasant. It's an event I will always treasure, for I was able to spend time with him even though it was only a friendly get together, he was the first who gave me that pleasure, though unaware, he wouldn't be the last. Through the coming years, I have met dozens of individuals that have made my eyes pop out of its socket in disbelief and my heart pump unceremoniously, just by the fact that they are the ones whose qualities I find mesmerizing.

At first, I wasn't very particularly interested with Anthony's younger brother, Bobby, since he was too young for me back then. He was around ten years old, and my desire was with his older brother. However, as he grew older and Anthony began his quest of staying farther away from his family and me as well, I find myself looking and wanting Bobby more, like I did before when I was into his brother, only it's a bit different. I started noticing him the time when his body was entering the stage of development and maturity, and a sense of complete turn around from what I used to know about him. Anthony was a little on the chubby side, yet still quite sexy and sensual for someone like him, but Bobby as I find out, was very much different. He was developing into a person devoid of unwanted baby fat and awkward physical side effects that comes along as one enters the stage of puberty. He was an Adonis in all aspects, and I was falling in lust over him, also at the same time, feeling a sense of envy and jealousy, for how can someone like him be so physically perfect and still manage to be as smart as I know him to be. He's very much aware of what's going on with his surroundings and the people living in it, unlike Anthony, who doesn't have a care whether someone was manipulating him like me, or anyone else for that matter. There were times that I can basically tell Anthony to do anything, and he would do it with no questions ask. Thinking he's in the best, possible care. However, I had something far more devious than what he expects; I used him in every form or shape you can think of. In order for me to have what I wanted from him, that is, to see more of his body, to make him do things that in my own advantage is an opportune moment to experience every fiber of his body, without going too far as to jeopardize my own. Nevertheless, I would rather have Anthony than someone who's aware of what I am doing to them, and Bobby knew that. He even asked me if I was hitting on him during the time, I was joyously cutting his hair, and unexpectedly my hands were on his bare shoulders supporting his head from moving. Thinking he would not have known such touch of affection, yet he did, and from then on, I was very much aware that he might be someone who knows my hidden agenda. However, that did not stop me from achieving my goal of being his friend, and we did became friends, until it was time for him and his family to move out of their house to a new one. A place where I won't be able to visit them or see Bobby half-naked every time he opens the door for me. So as my final gesture of affection to him, I went there one summer morning to capture, what would be my last time seeing his beautiful body on film. I was fortunate enough to have him on tape right before my eyes, to view his beautiful body whenever I feel the urge of missing him, to look at his perfectly, chiseled torso unbelievably for such a young age. He was sixteen when I got him on tape, for-ever capturing his youth on film, and running it whenever I needed, he is after all, the one who knows who I am, in a way, and somehow he made that day for me very meaningful.

Then there are others like him in between, although, they were just chance encounters with no real foundation, nevertheless, they provided me some moments where I could be with them, if only through imagination and fantasy. However, even if I had the chance to have intimate relationship with them, where I could fulfill my innermost desire with someone like them, I'll probably restrain myself from doing it, since I would surely end up in a very uncomfortable situa-tion and worst, may end up in jail. For my desires are from individuals who are not only physically unfit to be involve in such a mature relationship, but also emotionally incapable of understanding such concept, since they are still at a stage where they are searching for their own identity as an individual, living in a world full of flesh starved people. Therefore, what do I do when I can't have something I want sexually? Well, I'll just to look, stare, and imagine what it would be like to have someone like them with me all the time, acting like an anti-dote to a sexually starved person like me in order to satisfy my hunger. And as of now, it is enough for me to tame the beast within, yet I don't know how long I could keep it together without letting my inner struggle lash out and act on my desire to an unsuspecting victim.

Today, and maybe a couple years from now, I can still hold on to my sanity before I reach the final stages of what would become my terrible completion. I fear that when I finally become what I dreaded the most, I would have no control over it, rather be a slave and a reluctant watcher through the conscience I still possess. For only through my morality and strong faith that keeps me from doing what I wanted to do in the first place. I think I know that you know what I'm talking about, and where I'm leading. Problem is would I do something about it?

We shall soon see...

24

A LINE BETWEEN CONFUSION AND OBSESSION

This particular subject matter on the last chapter of the book I'm writing must be dealt with extreme sensitivity and caution, as well as detailed accounts of emotions I'm having. Hoping it will shed some light to me and for others, in order for them to understand what I'm going through every time I talk about the feelings I have with the people of the same sex. Like I've said before and many times after that, that I love guys who're not only cute and charming, but also possesses the qualities that I see in boys. Qualities that certainly a few of them have and many of the latter possess; smooth, clean, boyish and innocently unaware that they are the object of my affection. I like men, but I like boys too, yet it goes deeper than that.

Somehow, I've become acutely aware that I've been gearing towards boys almost all the time now, especially the moment I've arrived on this place, where there are an abundance of people I like and lusted for. These boys have been my constant relief in times of loneliness, or just from sheer excitement to see them. I'm not quite sure why I have strong feelings for them, in such a manner, that I too, still have strong feelings for the same person my own age, even older. But it's a feeling I can no longer ignore.

Pursuing such feeling would certainly make me not what I said I am, which is a homosexual, rather a person whose sexuality falls into a very different category, one that is suffering from a severe form of illness, where there is absolutely no cure for it. Moreover, if caught early on, will certainly be branded as someone who likes to be sexually satisfied by individuals who belong to a group before they reach the age of majority or maturity, I'm talking about boys' ages ten to eighteen years old, whose qualities I've described definitely falls into their category. The feelings I've talked about may not only involve affection, but also of a disease, with which, if acted upon will forever be branded as a child molester, a pedophile, a person who likes boys, one who can't do without thinking about them.

I am that person, and yet I disagree that I am that person. Confusing? So am I, yet when I think about it, I'm just following my feelings, the things I preferred when it comes to a guy, also at the same time, scares me since my preferences are getting younger and younger, to the point that I don't know the difference between lust and affection. Simply, to put it in perspective, wanting to be like them and desiring to have someone like them. I know that when I was younger, at the age where I'm trying to find my own identity and preferences, I discovered who I really am and what particular person that catch my attention. They were people of my own age, eleven to eighteen year olds, who at that time certainly would be normal, being attracted to your own age even if it meant that you have feelings with the same gender. That's what I am, and that's what I prefer back then, now that I'm an adult, I still have those preferences and the same feelings with me, and as strong as it was back then, it is still strong now, maybe even stronger. Whenever I look at them, I see someone not as a young person, a boy, but somebody that I wanted to have and be with. Moreover, the feelings gets stronger whenever I get to know them better and longer, I couldn't stop thinking that maybe, this is what it's supposed to come for me, that I'm destined to become someone who likes boys and who would do anything to be with them. Wherein the only way for me to be fully satisfied in one form or another, is to have a special attraction to young boys, one that I can never do away with, should I accept such ordeal? That I am forever will be attracted to them. Will I be able to suppress such feelings towards boys if I wanted to? I don't know, and I don't know if I want to. Is this what convicted and closet pedophiles struggle every single moment of every single day whenever they see a good-looking, charming, smooth and well-endowed lad pass by? But how can I be one of them, if I like a young person of the same gender that I discovered when I was a young boy myself, and carried that same feelings when I got older. Maybe, I become one of them if I acted on such feelings with any young boy that I like, yet I did that with Eric, the seventeen year old boy who gave me what I wanted the most in my adult life. One that I never had during my early years, because I was ashamed of who I am and afraid that people will disdain me for having the feelings towards the same sex, I was more ashamed and embarrassed than I was afraid back then, since peers dictates most of our social interactions. However, now I am more afraid than ashamed, because if I am caught acting on my feelings towards a boy. I'll be severely punished and will forever be branded as despicable and disgusting, a person who commits atrocity to children, not by murder or slavery, but much worst. For to them, I deprive the boys of their respect and innocence, the very essence that makes them who they are, since they believe that I take away from them something so scared that I can never be forgiven. This is what scares me the most, to spend eternity in the depths of hell when the time of reckoning comes.

I've always promised myself that I will suppress my emotions towards them, that it will be the final time for me to stay away from such an indecent proposal. It is to end in vain, for I can never help myself but to go against my better judgment, and be tempted to look and fantasize what it's like to have someone like them in my arms. To feel and be driven to their bodies like someone receiving a gift so special, that you can hardly contain yourself but be a slave to its grip, totally under its control, yet also keenly aware that what you are doing is going against your own morality. Somehow, you don't care since you've wanted this for a long time and you're willing to sacrifice everything you believe in, and accept any or all consequences, just to be satisfied with what they can offer. Have I gone too far? That I can never take back what I took from them, even if doing through imagination and fantasy. In high school, a time when my hormones were on overdrive, as well as my curiosity was predominantly abundant, I was lucky enough to have Denver to be my first experience, although, we just did what any other curious teenagers did in those days. Exploring the fascinating experience of oral sex, which I only did to him, and let me clear that nothing else happened, it was nevertheless, a heavenly satisfying encounter, one that'll stay with me for as long as I live.

With that experience, and even before the countless rendezvous I had with him, it was then I realized that I love boys. Maybe because, it was an age where young boys like me are curious about their sexuality, and are willing to explore the things their forbidden to do. The same things I've went through, only now I know what I want, and whom I want. However, in order for me to accomplish that, is for me to take away everything that I believe in, and let my lust take over no matter what the consequences it may bring. Surely, it would be an experience I will never forget, and surely, I didn't. The experience alone has provided me with a sense of completion, and a feeling that it may never happen again, unless of course, I abandon the very essence that makes me who I am into the person that brings chaos and dysfunction to my humanity. Therefore, do I just keep on hiding it from everyone, pretending it never existed? That what I'm feeling is just a normal behavior experienced by all people, especially for someone like me, that it will soon boil down and my true feelings for men will resurface. I'm afraid that it has resurfaced, that it has revealed to me that I am truly in for them and there's nothing that I can do about it, except, realize and accept the fact that I am indeed in love with boys.

So does that make me a gay who loves boys or a guy who loves boys? Hmn…

TO WINTER'S END

After all the things I've gone through, the events that made my life interesting and the countless situations I've encountered, and most of all, the emotions I've experienced. I am still not quite sure whether it's enough to know who I really am and what purpose I have to a life that no one seems to know how long it will last. All I know from all of these is that I am just supposed to live. To live a life however and whatever I want it to be, to mold the things into shapes and sizes I wish it to have, and to make decisions according to my own discretion. Hoping that it'll somehow make me a better person in a world based upon physical appearance and social upbringing, instead of character and social acceptance. A harsh reality to swallow, but it's what we live in for the moment, and until we can somehow wipe out any or all prejudices and biases with one another, we are to live in this world not knowing whether if we could do better. I know we can, and until that time comes, I will keep on trying to let myself be heard and be felt by one or by everyone, hoping they will someway, somehow understand what I've been trying to impart in their hearts and mind. That one day, we will all be together as one, and still maintaining a unique sense of individuality from one another with no regrets or shame from being scorned or rejected by others for who you are and what you have chosen to become. It is a day that I will cherish and remember always, but for now, my life is already on its journey to events I know not of, some have already transpired for others to know through the words I've meticulously placed in my book. Moreover, the other events will still come, waiting with eager anticipation, hoping that I'll still have time to put each one of them into words for others to remember me by. Another chapter that will surely be as interesting as the first one, I hope.

Wait and see…for now, this is the END.

0-595-27430-7